Woman *of* Color

Woman *of* Color

LATONYA YVETTE

Abrams Image, New York

For River and Oak
Love, Mommy

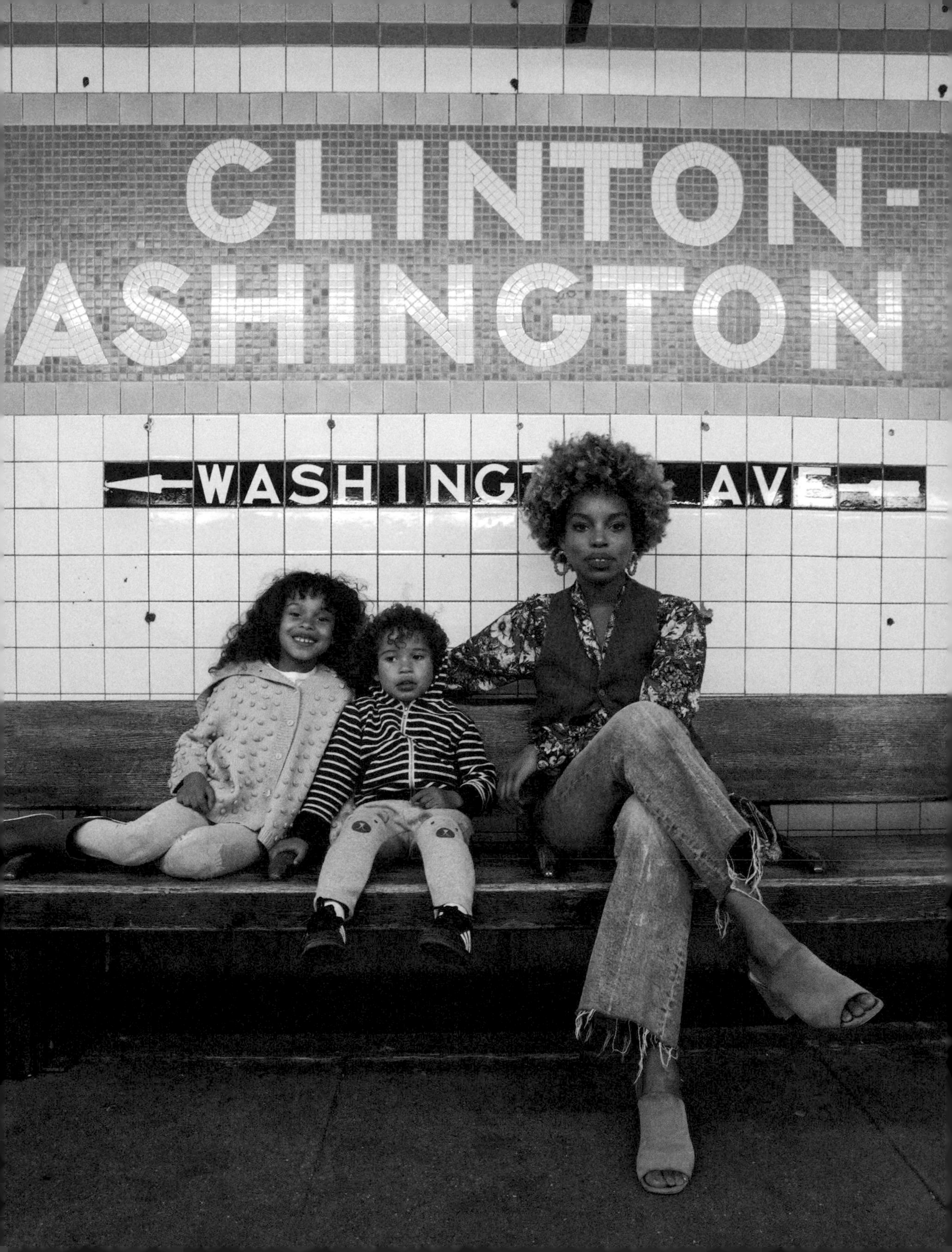
CLINTON-
WASHINGTON
WASHINGT
AVE

There are no photos of me from the summer I was born. I was dry and scaled. Brown and bald. Seven pounds and six ounces of unattractive bliss, caused by very little amniotic fluid, the bad luck of a twenty-three-year-old carrying her fourth child in the throes of an abusive marriage. I shed like a snake for weeks. My mother would touch me, and the dry outer shell that consumed my first few months of life would flake off. My mother says my due date was July 1, 1989. Then the fourth. Eventually, they induced on the fifteenth at Downstate Hospital in Brooklyn. All of my brothers and my sister have that dusty, pale hospital photo that plagued the eighties: pink bow. Blue bow. Striped Hospital blanket. Furrowed brow and cone-shaped head. Each of them, except me. While my mother thinks I was beautiful, the lack of photographic evidence mixed with the description of me as a newborn leaves little to help me imagine such. It is no surprise that I grew up questioning how we come to define beauty.

At that point, my dad should have been off drugs. My baby photos show my father with a wide smile, often sporting a drink in his hand. My mother: her large and beautiful forehead, her head of thick jet-black hair, and her eyes always communicating something more than what the lens intended to capture. My earliest memories are of her smiling and smelling faintly of Wind Song or Chanel No. 5. My dad's smile reached from ear to ear, his deep dark skin smoothing at the corners. Those first few years of my childhood, when we lived on Saint Marks Avenue in Prospect Heights, Brooklyn, were full of typical tropes of the eighties: plastic-covered white sofas, merlot turtlenecks, fur-trimmed leather coats. And babies with babies.

Today, I am not too far off this path. I had my daughter, River, when I was twenty-one, and then spent the next few years trying for my son, Oak. In all, my twenties have been dedicated to raising babies; this, together with my past, has shaped a version of beauty that is in constant evolution. I don't mean beauty as the physical or visual realm we often align it with; I mean a kind of beauty that exists in relation to, and because of, the ugly. The crack my father smoked. The beer he made me grab from the fridge, using me to sneak alcohol behind my mother's back that one summer in Silver Spring, Maryland. The same summer I jumped on his back, hitting him with my fists, in defense of my mother. The vitiligo that plagued me and filled my face with white fire at seven. The lupus that I assumed grew within my blood. The physical fights. The bullying. The births. The pain. The loss. The weight gain. The weight loss. The sight of my grandmother cold and still in her apartment when I was eighteen. But, also: beauty in the floral wallpaper she meticulously layered over and over again in her Classon Avenue apartment. The second kitchen she turned into a walk-in closet, filled with metallic suits, taupe and navy espadrilles, and men's blazers. Beauty in the window boxes full of flowers she sang to and tended each day. The Sundays when my mother sat me down on the hardwood floor, braided my hair, and sang me songs that comforted me throughout it all. The act of resistance in it—in choosing to see beauty through the grit each day. Beauty as resistance. Beauty as survival.

Clockwise from top left

I remember being so excited about that little dress. It was a Christmas gift along with the slippers.

My mom was–still is–big on Christmas, so it is no surprise that she took us to whatever Santa she could find. This one was a Rent-A-Center Santa, and, of course, I wore a two-piece floral sweat suit. Back then my mom bought me a lot of outfits like this, which I would wear together or mix and match. I loved them tremendously.

River and me on an Impossible Polaroid, shot by Peter in Bushwick, Brooklyn. We found that Ergobaby baby carrier at a stoop sale, and I loved the worn-in feeling of it and the way River would look up at me and we would be able to interact and have conversations. It helped balance the baby and me; I was able to wear clogs and heels and still feel like I had a bit of style while carrying her.

After River was born, I attended college for writing and literature and started my blog, *LaTonya Yvette* (originally *Old, New, and the Wee One Too*), as a place to document that beauty within style and motherhood. And I was proud that my blog occupied a predominantly white space. At first, I told our story without truly sharing my story. River was tiny and adorable and half white, and we spent many of our afternoons running around the city. Sharing our adventures felt unique, but soon, the blog became an outlet to connect with other women like myself: young, stylish mothers. Before the blog, all the other mothers I knew seemed to have planned their pregnancies. They gave up knit skirts for yoga pants and on-demand breastfeeding—and they had fifteen years on me.

      I was playing the blogging game until a very real and public experience called me on my bullshit. I had announced my second pregnancy and begun to document it on the blog by standing under Manhattan street signs that matched the number of weeks along I was. And then I lost the baby. While the weight of this loss was so personally layered, adding a public dimension required that I open up and truly honor the experience of grief. I wrote a short and sweet post explaining the baby my then-husband, Peter, and I lost, then another when it looked like our world had been pieced back together—when in reality, it hadn't. The supportive emails and comments that poured in stunned me. They cared for me during the day and when I couldn't sleep at night. They never really stopped. They helped me pull myself back together, but also required that I slowly lift the veil on the many nuances—whether style- or motherhood-related—that in and of themselves compose womanhood. Even with the transparent online shift that occurred after losing my baby, the stories I share in this book barely revealed themselves on my blog.

16

My second pregnancy, right before I lost the baby. Seventeen weeks, standing under a 17th Street sign in Manhattan. I did this as a way to document the weeks for my blog.

Clockwise from left

I had so much fun dressing River. In the early days I stuck to yellow and orange, and these were one of her first pairs of real tennis shoes, which she adored. We were on our way to buy a plant, and it was a chilly day, so I layered a basic outfit with an Ace & Jig duster.

Photographed with Oak a few days after he was born. I'm wearing my favorite muumuu and box braids.

I purchased this Quinny stroller from eBay when River was around four months. It was a pricey mistake, but, of course, I loved her in it. This was snapped on our first day traveling from Bushwick to Williamsburg. That tongue!

Before River was born, I would thrift a few pieces for her during my pregnancy. This continued until she was about four and started to ask to dress herself. This outfit was one of my favorites: a small felt-like dress with buttons paired with shorts and sunglasses that would flip up to reveal clear lenses. She would pull that green wooden alligator all around Brooklyn like it was a pet of hers!

Stoop fun with River in new kicks!

This book is about the growth of a young woman of color through the many phases of her life. But as I was writing, I realized that it is just as much about my family—my brothers, my sister, my mother, my father, my grand-mother, my uncles, and my aunts. Back then, everyone had a hand in raising me, and in defining the way I see and tell a story today. These are my stories in a sea of experiences that don't belong to just me.

Before there was a black girl creating a business and thriving in a world dominated by white women; before I chopped all my hair off in a hole-in-the-wall Dominican hair salon in Bushwick, Brooklyn; before the summer I fell in love with a white boy from Salisbury, Maryland; before I had my children, River and Oak; and, yes, before I lost the baby in between. Before the several moves in a matter of years; before the bullying and self-hatred; before my skin started to peel and give way to white patches—before all of that, I was born the fourth of a rowdy group of five, with barely three years between each of us. My brother Tony was the eldest, then DaMãar, Brittany, me, and Dario. Today, some of us live in Brooklyn, and some of us remain in Virginia, the last state where we were all living together. And—this is no exaggeration—there is not a day that goes by when I don't miss living with them. It's an odd feeling; not necessarily missing your childhood, but missing those who were part of it. It is in part due to my mother forcing all of us to care for one another, but using that care as a ground of existence. "You're all you have," she'd say, whether we were living in a fancy house or moving from one home to the next because we were being evicted. And at the same time, my mother relied so much on her own mother and on her siblings to help raise us when things got tough. My uncle bought us many of our expensive sneakers, and my aunt gave me my first Tommy Hilfiger belly shirt, which I wore at the West Indian Day Parade when I was no more than twelve.

Since I started my blog six years ago, every one of my collaborations has been woven out of, or been connected to, a story from my past. It is something I cannot escape. Something I do not *want* to escape. When I was a kid, words were a way for me to escape; for many years, I watched my mom write, and I would read her pages at the glass dining table or on the couch on a Sunday afternoon.

Clockwise from top

From the summer of 2009. I'm wearing a vintage shirt of my grandmother's and a fedora that I purchased at Peachfrog, a shop I worked at that year.

My grandmother, photographed on one of her "dress-down" days. She's wearing a vintage skirt, blazer, and glittery gold slides. Her hair isn't too curled here, which means she was likely wearing a vintage hat and had taken it off.

Me and my brother Dario in front of my mother's house in Maryland. This was the house she owned. It was also the time my vitiligo felt its worst.

Me and Dario at a fair that was hosted by my dad's job for the Metro Subway in Maryland. I picked out that green shirt and green skirt. I wore the outfit for years. I did that with many pieces of clothing because I gained very little weight as a child and could keep wearing the same ones.

When I became an adult, style was a way for me to create. I was seventeen and working at Skechers in Time Square, where, somehow between the swarms of tourists and overwhelming lights, I played around with the way the sneakers were lined up on a shelf or staggered them to make purchasing most optimal. Then there was my job at Esprit, where I often felt perplexed and frustrated by the visual team's lack of creativity. Why did the windows need to be created based on graphs and sales charts rather than on what drew people in with pure creativity? From there, I started assisting a soft-spoken German stylist named Sabina. I believe I always had it in me, but there was something about Sabina's honest and gentle encouragement, which was often tied into the realities of being a woman, a New Yorker, and, eventually, a mother, that felt like the necessary push to play around with style as a career. Later, while both of our careers kind of ebbed and flowed, Sabina was River's first babysitter and reassured me that I had all that River needed.

So much of my life can be seen through foggy, colorful, layered, and yet detailed snapshots around beauty and style; the stories in this book unblur the lens for me, and I hope for you, too. I have learned that clarity often happens in the moments when we share. Each chapter includes practical advice and lifestyle takeaways, serious and honest moments, and, of course, moments that are completely light and hilarious. And in this book, the sharing goes beyond just me, as I share not only my experiences, but those of other women of color. At the end of each chapter, I interview a woman, like designer Aurora James of Brother Vellies or doula Latham Thomas of Mama Glow, who in some way aligns with my essay. If I have learned anything from growing up, it is that no experience is only my own. Yes, the circumstances are unique to me, but often, there is a thin sliver of thread that ties all of us women and our experiences together. I hope this book serves as a guide for you, wherever you may be.

All in all, this is a love letter to women—mothers, daughters, hair stylists, photographers, artists, writers, sisters, friends, and, of course, black sisters. Sisters, who are all too often made to feel as if beauty—whether it be gritty, natural, or traditionally beautiful—is made only for the consumption and advancement of others. Here's to us and sharing all the stories that live within us and that are for us. I love you.

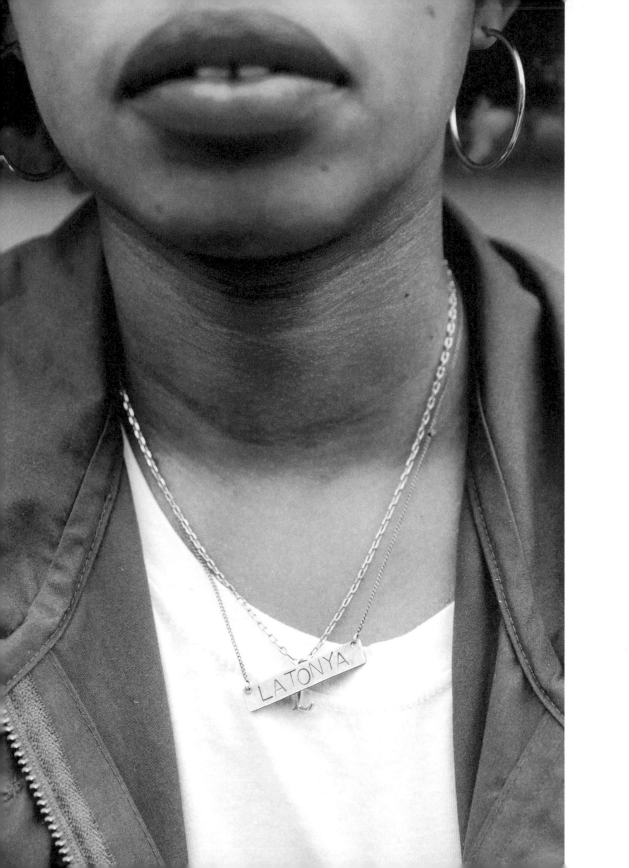

Chapter One
Tonya with a *La*

My family and childhood friends call me "LaLa" for short, but these days, everyone else calls me LaTonya. The nameplate necklace I never take off immediately gives my name away. The stamping on it is a bit haphazard and funky, in a way that is at once unclear and clear. The L and a are aligned, but the T is crooked and the o, n, y, and a kind of rise up, as if I am reciting my name, as if they are notes on a musical scale. A rise there. A Brooklyn accent here. An untraceable accent over there—an acknowledgment of the places I've been, the cities I've lived in, the neighborhoods within neighborhoods.

I loved this dress. School pictures were such a big deal, and I am happy my mother made them so. I do the same for my kids, and I remember feeling so beautiful with my hair curled and halfway up. I think I was in kindergarten here.

The necklace is now darker in color than it once was and held together by a tiny gold clasp twisted slightly to the left. Occasionally, it catches on a sweater, and I release it from its grip. After years of never taking the necklace off, I lost it in 2015 during a routine photo shoot at a loft in Greenpoint, Brooklyn. I took it off to be photographed and forgot that I placed it on a shelf out of sight. Months went by before I settled with the reality that I didn't know where it could be. I did something I often do when something may be too painful to digest—I waited. My therapist, Dr. Rose, calls it storing and sorting. That over there. That over here. I'll deal with this when I can. I think, in many deeper ways, it's how I've survived trauma.

I kept this heartbreak in the back of my mind throughout the summer of 2015. And then a friend with whom I had had an intense falling-out delivered the necklace to me one September afternoon on a park bench in the East Village as our kids played nearby. A subconscious peace offering. A resolution to all the things that were left unsaid between us. It is weird how a necklace with your name on it can be powerful. The gesture of wearing my name makes me think of the ways people take away and then add to who they are. Maybe more so, the gesture is an acknowledgment that we aren't really our names, that they are just attached to us. They are given, played with, celebrated, or resisted.

* * *

Throughout elementary and middle school, I wrote my name with a space in between the *a* and the *T*—*La Tonya*—declaring to anyone who would listen that my birth certificate mirrored my handwritten version. This wasn't just something that was questioned by teachers and classmates here and there. The correct spelling was something I continuously doubted for years but that I vehemently defended, so much so that at one point I began to put a dash between the *a* and the capital *T* for emphasis. *La-Tonya*. It wasn't until I was about fifteen that my mom attempted to convince me that *LaTonya* didn't have a space between the *a* and the *T*. I personally didn't believe her until I was seventeen and went downtown to the Department of Health and picked up a hard copy of my birth certificate. There it was. Just, *LaTonya*. It is one thing to be the fourth in a rambunctious group of five children—fighting for

Clockwise from left

At Disney World for River's sixth birthday.

Years after my first encounter with Ergobaby baby carriers, I got to work with them on a series for my blog. I wore my grandmother's beret and coat over the carrier to keep warm (and a bit stylish) that winter.

River hanging out after school. I love the way her newly cut bangs look with the rest of her hair.

the attention of your full-time working single mother. It is another thing to be given almost the exact same name as your mother—who was just *Tonya*—but the more "ghetto" and "unrefined" version. At least that's what my teenage self believed—a teenager already aware that blackness in America is generally equated with a lower class. Imposed structures, from the start.

Once I was done emphasizing the *a* and the *T* in my name and no longer imagining a space between the two letters, I started calling myself Tonya. I frequently opted to leave the *La* out when ordering coffee at a café, or when introducing myself to someone new in a big group. The *La* is frequently misheard as *Na*, and others usually try to spell it in front of me, in a clear subconscious—or conscious—attempt to more clearly align my name with my skin color. Back then, *LaTonya*, no matter which way I placed and replaced it, felt rough, overwhelming, and coarse. And yet to insist on a gap, to refuse to be aligned in these ways, allowed me to both celebrate my name—the necklace, the dancing nameplate—and to create versions of myself that allowed me the greatest freedom possible. I am, like my name, always on the move.

I have spent a few years navigating these funky in-between versions of myself and worlds as both a woman and mother. Whether involving my name, an interracial relationship, an internet space mostly structured for white women, or raising biracial kids, these experiences have all required not just a double consciousness, but a layered and complex one. Each time I would let the reality of the way the world saw me and my husband, Peter, (or us) slip, I would be reminded of it. When we tried to move around Brooklyn, it was clear that the presence of my white husband opened doors and gave us access to seeing apartments and rentals. It didn't matter that I was also financially providing. Landlords often wouldn't even speak to or see me until I had what I sarcastically called my "White Card." And there were also the months and years through which, on occasion, an older white woman assumed that I was the nanny and not the mom.

In the summer of 2010, Peter and I settled on River's name while sitting on a wobbly weathered bench in front of the restaurant Pop's in Williamsburg, Brooklyn. *River*, because I wanted and needed the transition into motherhood to be peaceful. *River*, because I also wanted to preemptively offer my daughter a path not predetermined by a specific gender. We

31

Clockwise from top left

River on her first birthday in our
Bushwick apartment, chewing on her
first birthday cake.

Breastfeeding Oak on a hot summer
day. I'm lying down in a more structured muumuu, of course.

Oak (a little over a year old) in his
stroller, drinking from his sippy cup
during a day out in our neighborhood.

lived on Wilson Avenue when I had River in 2011, then Clinton Avenue when I had Oak in 2014. Wilson Avenue was in Bushwick, and we were struggling to pay $1300 in rent for a third-floor walk-up. We moved to Clinton Hill three years later. We still struggled, but in our own creative fields and in our own way, and we were doing this in a neighborhood that, while rapidly changing, felt visually representative of our family structure, with mixed families of all kinds. A more privileged struggle.

I wore my nameplate necklace almost every single day. Through both seasons of life—my children caressed it as they nursed. Pulling and breaking and watching me piece it together again. I often forget that it's on me until one of River's friends loudly reads the tarnished thing across my chest—breaking down the *L*, *a*, and *T*. In those moments, I am no longer "River's mom." I am LaTonya. Oak calls me LaTonya when he's trying to test my limits, and I snap back into multiple spaces in time. LaTonya. LaTonya is the one raising you, yes. LaTonya is the one who now calls Brooklyn home with her kids. LaTonya has carried pain and joy. LaTonya is the woman behind the blog. Nothing in my life has stayed the same, and yet the name is still there, no matter how often I have switched it around.

∗ ∗ ∗

33

In the winter of 2018, on a sunny January day, I lay in my bed in the back of our Clinton Hill apartment. It is the quietest space in our home, overlooking our cement yard littered with plastic cars and tricycles. Oak lay beside me while my necklace crossed itself around my neck, landing on my shoulder. He tucked himself into the fold of my body. "O-A-K!" he often spells with confidence. He is in the season of his life where he seems to be finding his own way around his body and name. And I constructed his name during a time when I felt weak and broken from the baby I had lost before him. A time when I needed him and my pregnancy with him to be strong. When I first found out I was pregnant with him, my best friend, Lauren, told me about the oak trees that grew where she lived—their roots woven so deeply into the earth. Her town would have these terrible storms, but the oak trees would always remain, as if the world around them weren't

Clockwise from left

I spent many mornings and days with Oak during the first few years of his life, and this was taken for a blog post showing our typical morning. Here he is with his *yaya*–pacifier–which we couldn't get rid of. I love the way his body slumped into mine.

Post nursing, winter cuddles.

Oak playing in the gardens at the Pratt Institute on July 4. The vintage blazer was a gift from a friend.

Opposite

During the summer, the kids and I can often be found on the stoop, snacking or entertaining each other. Here we are in Fort Greene before heading to an outdoor movie at the park.

tossed up. I had never heard of a baby named Oak, and each time I closed my eyes, I couldn't stop calling him that. There was no alternative list of names, like other parents create during their pregnancies. I wasn't stubborn or uncreative; I just knew. And the shock around his name from friends and family left me unfazed. The intuition that Oak was his name was so strong within my body, and it was a swift decision, if it ever was one.

As we cuddled that winter day, he crawled his hand up between my breasts, tracing his fingers around the letters of my name on my necklace, as if he'd never felt it before. He has been tracing the same letters for years as a form of comfort, and in it, comforting me. We snuggled, and I realized that this necklace serves as a reminder of a woman and the stories held within her, how I've grown with my children and my name.

5 Rules for Coming into Your Own

1. The road to "coming into your own" requires an acknowledgment of all the generations that gave you a path to then explore what "your own" may even consist of.

2. Everyone has an opinion. None of it matters. Coming into who you are often takes an immense level of privacy.

3. Flaws are building blocks for what eventually sets you apart from the rest. Look at them with care. Use them to your advantage.

4. No one can put you in a corner if you don't give them a corner to put you in.

5. How everyone sees you is their problem. How you see yourself is yours. Work on that before you start working on how you're viewed by others.

Hannah Bronfman

DJ, Founder of HBFIT, and Entrepreneur

Hannah, the brand, fits under a broad lifestyle term that often doesn't encompass all that Hannah the woman does. She is a DJ who has carved out a permanent space for herself in the wellness/beauty/fitness industry. In short, she is a woman you want to know. She is a jack-of-all-trades.

I first met Hannah at a panel we were both on about fashion and entrepreneurship in 2017. That afternoon, as we were waiting for guests to arrive, the other panelists and I sat in a circle and started to kick around a few ideas to get us warmed up. Hannah and I were across from one another. The sun was bursting through the windows that encapsulated the enclosed roof, and at one point Hannah smiled at me, pulled out her phone, and snapped a picture of me, then continued chatting about her brand. When we were done talking, she showed me the photo, and we exchanged numbers. Within thirty seconds, Hannah broke down this wall that had invisibly divided us. She immediately became an honest part of the lifestyle and social media field, and we've been friends ever since. Here is our conversation.

LY Was there a specific time in your childhood that self-exploration felt heavy? How did you handle it?

HB It's funny, because I used dance as a creative outlet as a kid, but that's where I experienced most of my hardest realizations. Mostly about the shape of my body and the color of my skin, because I didn't look like everyone else. I must have been about ten years old, and the girls at Alvin Ailey told me that I didn't have enough rhythm to do modern dance and that I should stick to ballet. I felt like they were questioning my blackness. Then, when I was twelve years old, my best friend in school was mad at me because I started "dating" a boy she liked. I found her notebook in front of my locker, and when I opened it, she had written herself a journal entry, and in that passage, she called me the *N*-word. I was shocked. I didn't know what to do. I just remember being so scared to tell my mother because I knew how hurt she would be. I knew how hard she worked to make sure I felt confident in myself. She always told me that people would try to bring me down but that I needed to be strong because I had so much to offer the world, and people will always try to take that from you.

LY Was there a pivotal "moment" you felt like you came into yourself, or made it with your brand?

HB The digital network PopSugar came to me in 2015 to offer me my own digital show, called *Hannahgram*. I was really taken aback that they thought I was dynamic enough to hold my own show. I knew I was, but the recognition from them was dope. Having the episodes viewed over a million times was the cherry on top.

LY As a woman of color, what does this space you have carved out for yourself mean to you?

HB As a woman of color and someone who was constantly the scapegoat growing up, it's hard to really put into words what this means to me. I've had corporate jobs and worked in a few different industries, and I wouldn't have ever imagined when I was fifteen—nor when I was twenty-three—that I would be doing what I'm doing now. Now I feel like my power is *me*, the person, the brand, and I hold the cards to my destiny. My values have stayed the same, and as long as they do, the [limit to my] growth is unknown. I will continue to investigate the world of wellness and share all my knowledge with my community. It has been so rewarding to open doors for other women, particularly women of color in the industry. To all the people who told me I wouldn't amount to anything great—this one's for you!

43

"If I had a strong sense of self, I could deflect the words that may be used toward me in a negative way."

LY   **Has your family played a role in who you are right now?**

HB   My family has played an integral part in who I am today. My parents come from two very different backgrounds, and both have shared the pros and cons of those experiences with me over and over again. My mother was from a lower-middle-class family from the South Side of Chicago. She would say that her family life was less than supportive to her because she knew she wanted to be an actress, but her family constantly told her she wouldn't amount to anything. My father is a born-and-raised New Yorker and comes from a self-made liquor dynasty. He took over the family business despite the fact that he didn't go to college.

    They taught me at a young age that I was different, and that was my superpower. They told me that historically, my mixed race was something the world was still being introduced to, and that I needed to always know who I am because if I had a strong sense of self, I could deflect the words that may be used toward me in a negative way. They also told me I could do anything I wanted in life as long as it was to affect people in a positive way.

LY   **What's one lesson you hope followers and fans take away from you and everything you're doing?**

HB   No matter where you are in your life journey, you have the ability to change your own life for the better, and that change starts with you and no one else.

45

Chapter Two
Color Matters

My mind is mostly composed of snapshots;
clothes, patterns, colors, and textures are
often what I remember most. They are
like magazine clippings taped to a wall: a
red skirt there, a tank top here, my favorite
onesie over there. I see colors as leaflets
constantly fanning out in the front of my
brain. It's how I've always seen the world.
There is also a part of me that knows I see,
read, and remember this way because it
allows me to edit these details, or reshuffle
them—remembering too much can be
painful and overwhelming. It keeps trauma
out. It keeps joy in. It's carried me and driven
my creativity. More than anything, it has
protected me.

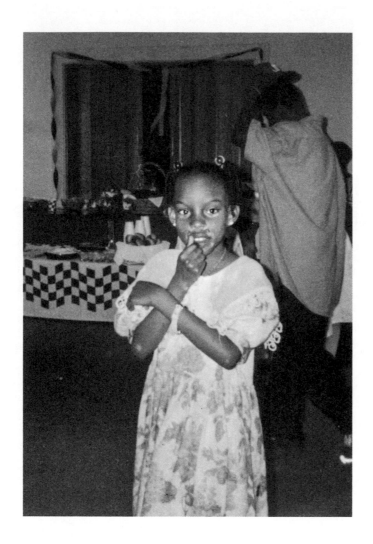

This was taken at my great-grandmother's
birthday party in Richmond, Virginia, when
I was seven or eight years old.

For the first day of third grade, my mom bought me a leopard-print vest, a polyester leopard-print long-sleeved shirt, and denim pants that had leopard-print fabric pleated on the hems. With the usual pile of jeans, skirts, basic shirts, one pair of sneakers, and one pair of dressier shoes she had purchased for me, that combo stuck out the most to me. I remember how the leopard pleats on the pants felt as I walked into school that morning. I hopped off of the bus, the vest close to my flat chest, the pants hugging my hips closely and sagging slightly on my butt and legs. I was skin and bones with clothes draped over, mostly. The outfit must have cost no more than thirty dollars, but the possibilities of styling it felt endless. Sometimes I wore the vest with a pair of my favorite jeans or over a red dress and knit tights that were so thick they sagged at the crotch a little. "Diaper booty," we'd call it. The pleated leopard pants were paired with a basic white shirt. The leopard shirt worn under one outfit or the next.

Third grade was different than the rest. We were in Maryland, because at one point, my parents decided to give it another shot, and Maryland was where they wanted to start again. And again. It had been a state I knew well, but a school system that always felt new. I felt eerily disconnected from the assimilation a child endures when going into a new year. I was guarded from the year before, the year the bullying was at its worst. I had been in the second grade then, and my uncle had bought me a bright yellow bubble coat for Christmas. That was the year I sat next to a girl who was plagued by eczema; her face, hands, and legs were raised, itchy, and chipping away. I loved all the quirky things about her. I liked the way her hand moved along with her pencil, and how the bumps on her thumb offset the orange undertone that lived beneath the yellow of the Ticonderoga pencil. Her clothes seemed pressed to perfection by her mother the night before: a plaid Peter Pan top, gray wool socks, pants that fit perfectly around her waist but seemed far too masculine for her height and shape. She was smart as a whip, confident, and highly uncomfortable. That year, it felt immeasurably relieving to sit next to someone whose body had turned on them in such an obvious way, too. My vitiligo was living. Her eczema was living. There was comfort in seeing her body and skin through her style and mine.

I was no longer sitting next to her after Christmas break. Our teacher had changed my seat because I laughed too much. Or laughed too loud. Both usually being the case. I wore the bubble coat on the first day back to school,

49

50

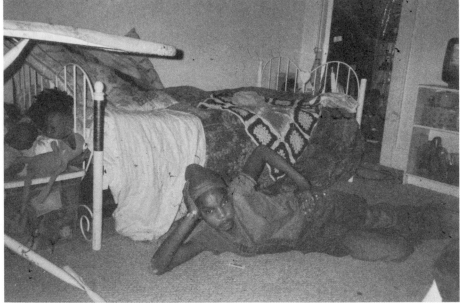

I used to get dressed and have my sister, Brittany, take photos of me with a disposable camera. I think I was around eleven or twelve in these photos. I'm wearing an orange do-rag, orange shirt, and Timbs.

and I now sat far from my friend who had been a mirror of the awkwardness of my body. Behind me was one of the more troubled kids in our class. I was her friend when she allowed me to be. But sometimes, I remained far too skinny, too silly, and overly aware to be. It was after Christmas when she wanted to build a friendship again—casually talking with me in line, asking me for a colored pencil from the red plastic pencil jar that sat smack-dab in the web that connected all of our desks. I obliged, and the friendliness was, of course, short-lived. When I wasn't looking, she and a male friend of hers found Wite-Out and wrote on my yellow bubble coat as it was on my body. I pretended I didn't feel it. I let the Wite-Out seep itself into the grooves of my new coat. When we were in line, I didn't dare to take the coat off or make it obvious that I knew what was on it. I pretended I didn't hear the cackling behind me as I walked around school that day. I knew that the coat had been marked; I knew that my own sense of freedom had then been violated.

It's weird how those things happen, how you allow them to happen. How you know as it is happening that that single incident will seep itself into the grooves of your body and brain, just as it did the coat. Throughout my life, clothes had this way of providing freedom in spaces and at times when I felt I wasn't free: a freedom of expression in the cream bonnet and red jumper I wore as a toothless baby in the crib in Brooklyn, in the white nightgown with pink florals I opened on Christmas morning when I was five, and in the green Converse sneakers and matching Celtics blazer I wore in middle school in Central Islip, New York. In that yellow bubble coat, too. How had I let my own freedom be stripped with my consent?

The year after that, the year of the leopard ensemble, I had a friend named Dana who wore a matching pair of Prada shoes with every top. When she wore a red pair, she would wear a fitted red T-shirt with a red, gold-buckled belt and braids with matching red beads. Her breasts always filled her T-shirts out, something I noticed in envy as mine barely afforded the chance to wear a real bra. It was almost spring of that school year by the time my body started to perk a bit—around the same time that my crush let me know that my barely-there titties were overshadowed by what he presumed to be my nipples. "LaTonya, you need to wear a bra. I can see your nipples!" he said with a unique blend of concern and laughter. The truth is, he couldn't have seen my nipples; they were tiny. He saw my large brown areolas. He hadn't seen anything yet; a little over a decade later, they would get darker and double in size after I got pregnant with River. Later that day, I told my mom, as if it had just hit me, "I should be wearing a bra!" And that weekend, she purchased my first training bra. It was off-white, lacy, and weblike, with a small pale pink bow that lay flat in the center. The straps were thick and itchy. And you should know, it never had the power to conceal my big-ass brown areolas. But, damn it, I finally wore a bra.

My mom didn't fight me on the bra. She never really fought me on anything beauty- or style-related. Though she was a fighter. Once, I snuck downstairs when I heard yelling, and saw my dad smash an egg over her head in a fight. She jumped back and grabbed a cast-iron pan, raising it to his head in self-defense. "I'm no punk!" she would often say if she was in a heated fight with my dad, or when reminiscing about her own fight-filled childhood. I knew she was tough.

There was this one time we were together when I heard "nigger-lover" yelled angrily by a stranger. I was no more than nine years old. I wasn't surprised by the way her body stood taller and tighter as she gripped my hand. I had an uncle and cousins and older brothers, so I'm almost certain I'd heard *nigger* in passing before. I was used to having Biggie Smalls, Jay-Z, A Tribe Called Quest, and the Wu-Tang Clan as a lingering soundtrack of my childhood, but that was the first time I felt like it was something to be ashamed of. The man said it to cut deep. So deep that I would feel the sting of the word years later. I still do. Hearing *nigger* spat from the tongue of a stranger speeding down a routinely crossed road is so different than hearing it dispersed into a few of your favorite lyrics by people who resemble you. That afternoon, she wore a red wrap dress that tightened at her waist. It swayed at the bottom to the beat of her hips. My mother looked good in about every shade of red, orange, or cream. Most often, she wore a bronze lipstick and a French twist held together by bobby pins. *Nigger*. Why was being a nigger a bad thing? And why was she called a *nigger lover*? She was my mother, and with everything I had in me, I identified her as a black woman like myself. Yes, she was lighter, but she was black. Wasn't she a nigger, too?

Some time before, while at a stoplight, the backseat of my mother's car filled with laughter when my brother Dario, who was about three or four, asked my mom if she was black. "Mommy, are you black? You look white." "Of course!" she said. His sincerity was hilarious. He went on to even question the shade of her skin compared to that of her five children. He was light-skinned, too, but not as light as she was. My oldest brother, Tony, was dark brown, my brother DaMãar a lighter shade of brown, Brittany lighter than DaMãar, and I was darker than Brittany, except for the bright white vitiligo that, if we count it, made me lighter than them all.

The color of my mother's skin was a point of contention my entire childhood. It was why she wasn't invited to visit my father's family when her children were. And, it was why we all didn't go. My mother being left out meant that all five of us would refuse in her honor. It is also one of the reasons we believe my father's family posed her as a woman out to ruin him. It wasn't the drugs he did in the eighties, the alcohol abuse in the nineties, or the physical and emotional abuse and the cheating the years in between. At the root of it all, it was my mother's complexion. The demons my father faced were just a result of being with a woman like her; she was not enough for a dark-brown-skinned, smooth-like-butter first-generation Panamanian man.

My mom's own mother was indigenous and black with bronze skin and high cheekbones. Her dad's lineage traced back to an interracial relationship that had once found safety in the streets of Brooklyn. To deny that being the darker brown daughter didn't cause a current of tension between my mother and me—competition, even—would be to deny what many other young black women often struggle with, right at home. And so, I won't. Colorism is something we know to be true within the black community, and something we rarely openly discuss. And shades of color, whether it be in China, the Caribbean, France, or America, are always judged as least to most preferable from darkest to lightest as the framework of beauty.

* * *

I am drawn to the way bold colors scream and pour themselves off of a body. My vision is funneled in this way, and maybe it is my own insistence on being seen no matter what—a refusal to conform—that is tied into wearing reds and oranges. Or maybe it was the way my mother looked

Above Me and Peter on our wedding day, photographed in front of the Brooklyn Museum. I'm wearing my grandmother's dress, which I added a train to for the day.

Opposite From one of my first dates with Peter in the summer of 2009. I wore an orange H&M dress with my grandmother's vintage YSL necklace and street bangles, and I had a bowl cut.

in red that drew me to those shades in the first place. So it is no surprise that one of my most memorable dates with Peter, from the summer of 2009, was the day I wore an orange H&M sack dress that I had found tucked in between jersey shirts and denim pencil skirts on the $5 rack. I cinched it in at the waist with a vintage belt and wore signature gold bangles with African tribal prints stamped on them. One dollar would get you about four of them anywhere on Flatbush Avenue. (Gold bangles are a Brooklyn girl's rite of passage. Before she was born, River had a pair tucked in her room from my mother. They are a mandatory style statement if there ever was one.) The orange sack dress matched my summer tan, and my body melted in it. That evening we climbed to a rooftop; the dress was tucked under my knees, and a cloud of weed surrounded Peter and his friends. The sun dipped low behind the buildings in South Slope, and I kept getting up to lean over the ledge and see the city from above. Peter had just moved from Maryland. There was a new Brooklyn shaping up. One that consisted of higher rents, older generations moving out, white people moving in, and the first round of high-rise buildings sprouting up. I had known nothing of it.

That same summer, while lying on a blanket in McCarren Park, Peter asked why I covered the big white patches on my knees, whether it was with clothes or Dermablend. I didn't have an answer. I didn't know why I kept covering the discoloration. As a twenty-four-year-old white man, he found the white patches on my black skin interesting. He never asked me why they existed; he just let me know in his own weird way that they were cool. I never covered up again.

After that summer, the color of us kind of became this distant thing. The clothes changed; I went from the orange sack dresses to blue blazers to a cream lace top that miraculously fit over my pregnant belly during the summer of 2010, when I celebrated my twenty-first birthday in Coney Island. The following summer, on our wedding day, I wore my grandmother's off-white lace dress with beads down the center as our daughter looked on. The dress was pleated and calf-length, and weeks before my wedding, I spent days sourcing replica lace to add a train. Years later, the dress hangs in my closet, waiting for the train to be removed and to be worn on a nice summer day. As I've grown, the color and snapshots seem to get louder, brighter, more complex. I mourn the possibility of no longer seeing the world this way.

5 Rules for Being Bold in Life

1. Limits are made to be pushed. If you believe in what is on the other side, keep going. Keep pushing.

2. Too often, women of color are made to feel they need to carry everything—job, friends, family, kids. Don't. Dictate what needs to be done and how, and don't be afraid to divide and conquer. Superwoman is not real.

3. "Attaining balance" is a myth that keeps women doing too much and yet expecting things to feel right. Going for it means just going for it; it doesn't happen when you're busy trying to maintain something that is not constructed to allow women to thrive. Everything sucks at one particular time or another, so what are you going to do about it?

4. Keep a set of politics that cannot be moved or reconstructed within or around spaces formed by others.

5. Put the oxygen mask on yourself before putting it on anyone else.

How-to
Turn Seven Core Pieces into Four Outfits

There are days when getting dressed feels as if it is some fraught task. Add color and texture to a wardrobe, and the task can feel larger and even more complex. In reality, incorporating color and texture into one basic look can make getting dressed *easier*, even fun. We shouldn't see clothes as things that are meant to restrain us, but as objects meant to, in many ways, free us—whether they're new, vintage, patterned, or will later be tossed. Here's how I take seven pieces and turn them into four outfits throughout the week. Get weird. Have fun. Be bold. What else are we to do?

The Seven Pieces

1. *White T-shirt*
2. *Vintage Levi's*
3. *Orla Kiely pink dress*
4. *Vintage red dress*
5. *Hackwith Design House wrap top*
6. *Vintage red trousers*
7. *Vintage jean jacket*

1   *Orla Kiely dress*
A basic white T-shirt
Vintage Levi's

For this look, I play around with transparency and color to create a soft, feminine boldness. The dress came with a slip, but I removed it, which gave me some space for creativity with the function and structure of the outfit. Often, something that is sheer feels intimidating if purchased outright. I recommend buying pieces that can be taken apart like this. The shoes are Brother Vellies and are an everyday, functional item that adds a bit of spice. If you take something that is bold in color and sheer, but style it with a basic look—jeans and a white T-shirt—you'll get comfort with minimal effort.

63

2 *Vintage dress*
   A basic white T-shirt
   Vintage Levi's

For this outfit, I experiment with color and pattern to make a bold statement and give off a bohemian and creative energy. The cool thing about wearing an open colorful or patterned dress is that it gives the outfit movement. This is essential if you are worried about getting swallowed up in a patterned look. I bought this dress for no more than $10. Originally, it had long sleeves that belled at the bottom, but I cut them and now often roll them up. Look for similar styles at your local thrift store, and don't be afraid to cut, unbutton, or roll up any part of a look so that it feels right for you.

3   *Hackwith Design House wrap top*
       Vintage Levi's

Here, we move back to basics and pump
them up with color through the accessories.
The design of a top like this—it's reversible—
allows the look to completely change
depending on how it's worn or what colors
it's paired with. If you're looking for an
easy way to add color to your wardrobe,
accessories are a great starting point. Stick to
what you know, and play with either the top
or bottom of your outfit (e.g., a hat or shoes).
My orange hat and earrings are the source
of color here. The balls of the earrings are an
odd contrast to the deep V-neck of my wrap
shirt. Normally, if I choose a big earring, I'll
skip a necklace. Or I'll go for a thin one like
my nameplate or something similar. Shapes
can be played with in accessories as well as in
the clothes. They allow the accessories to be
what speaks the loudest in the overall look.

4   *Vintage red trousers*
Basic white T-shirt
Vintage denim jacket

For this look, I play around with just one
big, bold statement piece. And as nerve-
racking as this may seem, it is actually the
easiest route of all the outfits. If you just
buy one bold pair of pants (e.g., orange,
yellow, or green) and style it with other
simple pieces, you have an easy entry into
bold style. It just takes a bit of courage. I
found these pants at a flea market, and they
were $5! I didn't even try them on. I just
knew they would be easy and worth the
manipulation if needed. Sometimes it just
takes a bit of boldness, imagination, quick
thinking, and color!

Aurora James

Founder and **Designer, Brother Vellies**

Aurora James is the founder and designer of Brother Vellies, an accessories brand that sustains the art of traditional African footwear by hiring artisans in Ethiopia, South Africa, Kenya, and Morocco to make shoes and handbags. While Aurora tested a few roles before she began her journey with Brother Vellies, she has made monumental waves as a designer and woman of color.

Meeting Aurora was one of those very New York things where you float within the same space for a while without actually meeting. We officially met at a dinner party with mutual friends. She talked about sparkles, and to be honest, I was taken aback by her level of confidence as a young black woman at a table with well-established white women from the fashion scene. It seemed as if she wasn't aware . . . or, rather, she was, and was willing to overlook that color could be something that divided the women at the table. Instead, she saw the night as an opportunity to bring a variety of women together. Here is our conversation.

LY How did you identify yourself as a kid?

AJ I grew up in Canada, so the concept of self-identifying was really different. My father was born in Ghana. My mom was adopted at birth, but she believes that she's Inuit and Irish. So, I don't know. I always felt Inuit, Irish, and Ghanaian, which I guess changed for me when I moved to America, because then people just identified me as being black, which took some getting used to but was also OK. It strips you of your culture in a lot of ways because being black is an expression, yes, but there's a lot of different types of black.

LY **How has this identity differed from childhood to adulthood?**

AJ Part of my childhood I also grew up in Jamaica for four years, which was a completely different experience, as well. My biological father was from Ghana and had a much more African perspective on his blackness than my stepfather, who was Jamaican but identified much more as being African American. He had a very different idea about beauty and white perceptions of black culture . . . which I think was also kind of jarring to me as a young person. He was like, "If you stay in Jamaica, then you can be Miss Universe Jamaica, but if you go back to Canada, then you're just gonna work in the grocery store." And I was like, "Well, why? I'm so smart." And he said, "Because white people don't care about black people." I would say, "Oh, I think you're projecting." I didn't actually believe what he said, but I thought, "Oh, there's some people who have that experience."

LY **Has being black become a part of your work in any way? And if so, how do you see it progressing?**

AJ I would definitely say that being black is a narrative in my work. My grandmother was also from Ghana, and she used to do this thing in the eighties where you sponsor a child for less than the price of a cup of coffee a day. But she sponsored lots of children; like, every day she would sponsor another child. It was actually really remarkable. I make jokes about it, but, you know, there were a lot of kids who subsequently would come to Canada and visit us, and she paid for some of them to go through higher education, which was also really phenomenal. . . . And I was pen pals with all of these kids growing up. . . . They were various ages, and what I realized is, some of them were living completely different day-to-day lives, but we still had a lot of the same coming-of-age struggles. So really early on I learned that even our differences connect us. . . . And "Africa" never felt as far away to me as I think it did to a lot of other people, because I had that shared experience with them.

When my grandmother passed away in 2004, I really wanted to do something to honor her. . . . [My mom] told me that old adage: "Give a man a fish, and you feed him for a day. Teach a man to fish, and you feed him for a lifetime." She said, "Why don't you focus on that idea, as it pertains to your grandmother's legacy, instead?" My grandmother was really big about the educational portion of sponsoring children; that's why she paid for a bunch of them to go to the University of Toronto. . . . Three years later, as I was traveling in Africa . . . I just became really enthralled and fascinated with their artisanship

73

"It's nice to have a multisensory experience with color. And I feel like that's why sometimes when I think of black and blackness, I also think of that as a multisensory experience."

there, and I realized that a lot of them were losing their jobs because everyone wanted to wear what David Beckham was wearing versus their own traditional cultural apparel. The secondhand donations that were coming from America were basically just undercutting their local ability to manufacture and sell product. So, I really wanted to try to create job opportunities for them. My work definitely does relate back to my black history.

LY **When I say the word *color,* what is the first thought that comes to mind?**

AJ Lavender.

LY **Why lavender?**

AJ When I say *lavender,* it's as a knee-jerk reaction. I actually picture the plant versus the Pantone. It's nice to have a multisensory experience with color. And I feel like that's why sometimes when I think of the idea of black and blackness, I also think of that as a multisensory experience.

LY **Tell us about a typical Aurora James outfit that combines color and general "Brooklyn stoop" energy. What does that outfit entail?**

AJ I love my stoop. A lot of my clothing is vintage for a lot of reasons. Number one, vintage stores are closer to me. Number two, I don't like shopping in [big-box] stores . . . I like to dig for things. I love color because I think color is a form of expression. I definitely go through monochromatic color phases, which are probably tied to something, but I don't think I have ever really delved that deep into that yet. And I wear a lot of dresses, 'cause I feel more free in a dress.

LY **How do you feel like Brooklyn aligns with that?**

AJ I think Brooklyn allows me to actually be myself a little bit more. Growing up, it was a little bit of a challenge, because I would wear what I felt like wearing and people would think it was super bizarre. I don't really feel that as much now, like I can just wear whatever and people will kind of be more at peace with it. I think that now instead of feeling like an outlier based on what you wear, there's almost an element of protection.

LY **If you had any last word of advice for little girls or women with similar backgrounds and stories like yours, what would it be?**

AJ I really live off of this amazing Margaret Shepard quote: "Sometimes your only available transportation is a leap of faith."

Chapter Three
La Pérdida

It was spring of 2012 when I took my styling on the road. River was a year old at the time, and we lived in Bushwick, Brooklyn. A year prior, the weight of my hips felt too heavy at 145 pounds when riding in a livery cab on Wilson Avenue, my back contractions competing with potholes in the dead of winter. I was 121 pounds at six weeks or so when my pregnancy was confirmed by my gynecologist on Park Avenue in Clinton Hill, and I had been 117 pounds the last time I weighed myself in my first apartment on Saint James Place.

36С   045   5H211103

My favorite one-piece that I burned a hole through. It was airy and the bottoms of the pants swayed when I walked. I felt so proud to wear it that picture day in first grade. And, of course, with a matching scrunchie!

My life, for the most part, felt like it had been surrounded by loss already. Of equal importance, often a gain is swiftly couriered in before the weight of loss has time to settle. Trauma is shuffled to the back. Queue the bright lights! It is the story of my life and that of others who are often plagued with trauma but also have enormous privilege. Bringing that experience of what is lost and what is gained into my approach to styling for women felt like the only way.

While I didn't have many clients when I first started out, the ones I had took energy and time and became intense and layered relationships. To go into a woman's closet and touch things that hold stories, or to assess why she has fifteen pairs of shoes and only wears two, or why she hides a stack of size 4 jeans when she is a size 8, takes nerve and care. Normally, a client's response would be a mix of concerns, confusion, and appreciation. My approach was to walk through it with them, and to reassure them that I am not doing something *to* them. I have learned that women tend to hold on to more than we need: clothes and people. I would always start every session by asking *why*. Why did they need me? What position of life were they in? What was the story they were trying to let go of? And who were they now? Doing that work while living through my own trauma was heavy.

The pieces of my own childhood outfits I wore and lost and the people who were there along the way are weaved into the threads of my clothes and my body. Thread by thread. Point by point. Like the outfit I wore in one of my favorite school photos: a red onesie with tiny white hearts printed all over. It had short sleeves and straight-leg pants. I lost that red one-piece when I attempted to iron it one morning. A cotton towel spread across my twin-size bed, my knees on the floor, the iron full of water. Turn on, heat up, switch to cotton, let it steam, then press down. A routine I'd known well. One morning the iron stuck—residual gunk from someone's something or another. It was too hot and the gunk was too much and I burned the pants. A hole in the left leg, the edges of it brown and charred, and a deep gut sigh released itself from my tiny body. Nearly a decade later, in the summer of 2009, I found a similar red one-piece while thrifting at the Goodwill on Fulton Street. It had shorts and long sleeves and was just $2.99. I cut the crotch out of the shorts, making it into a skirt, and ripped the sleeves off. The bosom was large, but it was loose, and I belted it with a mustard belt with a tortoiseshell buckle—one of my grandmother's, of course.

79

My father died soon after I thrifted that one-piece. It was the fall of 2009 when the air and leaves started to change, the unshakable respite from a sweltering Brooklyn summer and the distinct buzz of something new in the city air. I was staying with my mother in Bedford-Stuyvesant the morning we found out. I had gotten a message on Facebook from my cousin: "Hi LaTonya, I'm sorry to tell you this, but your dad died this morning." She left her number and ended the message with her name. My mother and my father were married for fifteen years but had spent much of that time on and off. They were divorced when he died, and it had been the longest stretch I had gone without seeing him. Five years before, my mom read an email from him while standing at the thirty-minute computers in the library in Richmond, Virginia. His letter to her was long, and I stood beside her as she read it. All I remember seeing was his name, *Franco*, and the word *cancer*. The other words within the email blurred before my eyes.

Within a few weeks' time, we were headed to Baltimore, Maryland, where my father was recovering from his surgery; inches of his intestines were removed to stop the cancer from spreading. The day we arrived, he wore a yellow T-shirt, a far cry from the deep blue button-up that my memory often places him wearing. The color of his skin, the wave of his short hair, and his dark pants always made him look like velvet. When we arrived, he didn't look like he had cancer, or that he was recovering from a surgery. I remember his smile, how it lit up and how I thought he was so beautiful. Just beautiful. I don't know of anyone who thinks their dad is beautiful, but he was. He lay down and I saw the scar reaching from the bottom of his belly up to his chest; it cut through his birthmark that matched mine. It was something that always connected us. He was in pain but alive and well. Optimistic and angry. My mom had packed us up and brought us to his side, so we all could be near him and she could care for him. Something she'd always do. I loved my father, but I hated being there. I loved my mother, but her desire to be loved by him in a way that was as temporary as it had always been made me resent her. The urgency of our visit, the lack of transparency on his part with his own family about my mother and about us, left tension so thick that our stay was my mother's

Top We stopped at a Wendy's on our way to Baltimore to visit my dad after the news of his diagnosis in 2013. I brought my camera, and my sister, Brittany, snapped this photo of me.

Above Me and my dad. This was taken when we went to visit him at his job. My mom matched my bo-bos to my top, and I wore these blue metallic sneakers/oxfords that had a slight heel. I was obsessed with them!

last straw. To this day, Baltimore is a hard city to visit. It was the last place I saw him alive.

Throughout my childhood, my father spent many years in and out of contact with us; then one day he would show up with a court order for visitation. Then he would be gone again. One afternoon during one of the visits, he turned to me and said, "I don't have to call, LaTonya. You can call me sometimes, too." I was around ten. He was serious. I have spent the better part of my twenties coming to terms with the fact that I won't ever fully understand my father's mind. And in all honesty, I think my mom spent some of the same years accepting that she kept chasing his ghost. In his death, I suppose, he chose not to run. Just to hide. He talked to my mother weeks before he died. She asked him how he was doing; he asked to come visit her; she declined. They wished each other well, and he told her he loved her. A few weeks later she sent him pictures of my sister's son, my brother's son, and me with Peter. "A white boy! Of course," he responded playfully.

He died weeks later. He knew he was dying when they talked and emailed. I made several calls the day he died, one to his own mother. By the time I reached her, the cremation process was just a few hours away. His memorial service, a day after. His mother laughed when I asked if my family could at least have his ashes. Collectively, we decided to skip his memorial. We weren't welcome. Brooklyn felt like the real place to celebrate him. It was the place he and my mother met, where they were married, and where most of us were born. We drove to Coney Island and sat in the sand together. We dug our feet deep into the cold September sand, locked arms, told him we still loved him, and said farewell to our dad.

* * *

My grandmother was tiny and soft-spoken, and one of the very few times I saw her manner shift was in reference to my father. One summer, he had pushed hard and won visitation in court (which he only followed through with once, because he said we hated it), and my grandmother became a facilitator of the visit. I could sense the weight of his actions in that swift transition of us from her to him. That's one of the very last times I saw their worlds cross before she passed away.

My grandmother on her birthday. This was typical.
She got dressed up, wore a crown, and had her photo
taken. The flowers were probably from my Uncle
Ronnie. She wore the crown every single birthday.

When my grandmother died, my father called my sister to let her know how sorry he was, knowing how much she meant to her and my mother. To all of us.

My grandmother was my style icon. Every so often I stumble upon a picture from the eighties or nineties of my grandmother wearing clothes I received after she passed away. While her collection was far too large for us to keep everything, in the wake of her passing, I had the opportunity to sort through her clothes and take what I could. There were men's vests and tulle skirts, a floral hatbox full of hats and scarves. There were some of the fanciest dresses I'll ever own, that she'd wear on a very normal day. There were boots and loafers, and even a pair of leopard high-waisted pants that fit like leggings. I've worn most all of it since she died, stitching a piece of her memory not just into my closet, but into my everyday walk in life.

Truthfully, though my grandmother was my style inspiration, I don't think I was the best granddaughter. I loved her and we talked, but I wasn't a caregiver like my sister or mother. Once, during a routine physical therapy session, she and I bickered a bit because I refused to let her be dishonest with her doctor about how "good" she was doing. My grandmother was the type of woman who drank natural herbs in the morning, spent an hour in prayer, and slipped into a pair of mildly stretchy gold stylish flats, even when her foot was swollen and wrapped in an Ace bandage and she could barely walk. I was bossy, and her resistance to healing or figuring out the source of her issues bothered me. It made helping her frustrating. She was so young. Why didn't she want the answers to live a more fulfilling life?

The morning she died, my mother called several times from her office, asking me to check on her. She was living on Jefferson Avenue, which was about a seven-minute bus ride from my mother's apartment. It was my first day off from work in a while, and I was hesitant to visit her. My grandmother was caring for my cousin, my aunt's son, full-time. When my mom had called earlier, he'd told my mother that my grandmother wouldn't wake up.

When I entered her apartment, she was lying on her orange couch like she always had. Her long brown hair beside her face with a blanket over her. The TV in her view, her side table full of things, a hatbox in the corner, a vintage lamp on the antique nightstand in the window. My cousin

jumped above her, planting his body on the top of the sofa back. "See, LaLa, I kept trying to wake her." I laid my hands on her chest. I'd never performed CPR in my life, but what do you do when your grandmother lies lifeless? You perform CPR. I interlocked my fingers and pressed my hands on her chest. She hardly moved. I whispered in her ear, "Please wake up, Grandma. Please wake up. We need you." I pumped again. And again. I grabbed my cousin and told him to go to his room and answer the phone that had been ringing off the hook. Someone knocked on the door and I let them in. It was chaos. My mother arrived, and I watched her perfectly applied makeup run in the living room while the weight of her body lay over her mother's. She was angry at me. At my grandmother. At everyone. My mom lost her mother that morning, and in some way, I think I lost my mother, too.

Where the fuck do dead dads go? What about dead grandmothers? They were both so young. Where do I find all the people I've lost? I've spent so much time talking and teaching others how to edit and let go. I've spent so much time on lessening the weight of garments lost to make space and time for the joy and creativity in getting dressed. Yet, I have not made peace with all the people I've lost in the process. I know they're in the clothes, but they aren't clothes. I wish they'd all just come back home.

Top My aunt (left) and my grandmother (right). This was taken either after church or at a party.

Above My jewelry is a mix of old and new, passed down and found. There are earrings from my grandmother and things from women-owned brands that have been sent to me over the years. I love that I can pick up something and know who gave it to me or where I was emotionally or physically when I got it. Even though my closet can get a little disorganized, everything is intentional.

5 Rules for Continuing to Heal from Loss

1. Grief has no expiration date. It doesn't magically disappear and there is no set of steps that then cure the loss of someone. You sometimes get better with it. Sometimes, it hits you right in the gut and forces you to lay it all down. Kneel, my friend.

2. Your version of grieving doesn't look like your partner's, mother's, sister's, or friend's. It can feel isolating, but remember that the face of such a tremendous feeling is unique to each person it overcomes. Be soft with those you love.

3. It's OK to talk. And keep talking. If there is someone willing to listen, let them. If you can write, write.

4. When you are forced to remember who you've lost, whether it be in the face of a stranger or in a quirky odd thing that only you two shared, steal those moments. They can hurt, but count them as joy.

5. Professional therapy is a great tool to have in your toolbox. If you have the means, please don't be afraid to use those who are trained to help. There are plenty of free hotlines and community-run programs that focus on grief. Though they aren't as intimate as a therapy session, they still are powerful and help create community.

How-to Purge Your Wardrobe

Whenever I am purging a client's wardrobe (or my own), I make them ask three questions when assessing each piece. Then, we decide what to let go of and what to keep. Ask yourself these questions when working with your own closet.

1. *When is the last time I wore it?*

2. *Are there three events or instances that I can wear it over the next two weeks? And if so, where and how?*

3. *Why am I holding on to it? What story does it hold or what story am I hoping to create in it?*

Sade Lythcott

CEO, the **National Black Theatre**

I met Sade at a dinner party hosted by our friend Sarah Sophie Flicker more than two years ago. We sat next to one another, and I was mesmerized by the way she spoke with passion on just about Every. Single. Topic. Sade's work streams within a bloodline of legendary Harlem-proud activism celebrating the arts. She's the kind of real New York woman full of grace, power, and a wealth of knowledge. She talked with her hands and kept me entranced. Through the years, we've kept in touch while her world has expanded with a new marriage and a baby and plenty of wonderful and meaningful work in between. Here is our conversation.

LY   Your life is so full, but when you think of the word *loss*, what immediately comes to mind?

SL   I equate the word *loss* to an emptiness—a sense of grief. The unreplenishable. There is a permanence to the word as I have come to know it. I guess I'm not positive that things lost can ever be found. As dark as that may sound, it is the thing that gives me the most peace in dealing with loss. Loss has its place. It is to be acknowledged, honored, not swept under the carpet or run from. It is the honoring of loss, the making sacred, that helps you heal, move on, and rediscover or come into a new relationship with whatever the void is. It is the *heart* work of this ritual that allows us to be the most free.

LY   How has this view of loss impacted your personal life and your work?

SL   The sudden loss of my mother (who was also my best friend) was devastating. The shock of her passing rendered me helpless, hopeless, and stuck in both the past and her passing. Life after loss is never the same, and reaching for it to be only retraumatized me. What I had to learn for my life and ultimately my work was that the universe is always conspiring for our highest good, whether we understand it in the moment or not. You must allow yourself to *feel* the loss as a part of your journey, not as a destination. Let it flow through you in order to steward you to where you were meant to be. My mother's passing has stewarded me into the fulfillment of my life's work at the National Black Theatre. It was by honoring my loss (instead of preserving it, which was my first impulse) that I ultimately found my way back to me.

LY   Now that you have a son, has this loss transformed?

SL   Being a mother has absolutely shifted my relationship to all things . . . in profound and unexpected ways. No one ever really talks about the deepening of relationships with the ones we have lost, but it can absolutely happen. I feel like through the birth of my son I have come to know my mom and her choices in a new and profound way. There is a sweetness to knowing that she is Thelonious's guardian angel. If I deal with loss at all since becoming a mother, it has more to do with wrestling with the loss of my old self.

LY   **It often feels like black women are supposed to carry what is lost and what is gained for an entire family or community. Do you feel like this is true, and is there any advice you can give for a woman of color who is currently going through this?**

SL   There is this amazing young Nigerian poet named Ijeoma Umebinyuo whose work I love. She has this one poem [published in her 2015 book *Questions for Ada*] that says:

> *Bless the daughters who sat,*
> *carrying the trauma of mothers.*
> *Who sat asking for more love, and*
> *not getting any,*
> *carried themselves to light.*

I think this poem speaks volumes to the weight of what we carry as women of color. My advice is simple. Always and in all ways: Travel light. Keep reaching for the light. Be the light. And remember to let kindness, patience, gentleness, and grace light your way as you journey into finding and falling in love with yourself.

97

"You must allow yourself to *feel* the loss as a part of your journey, not as a destination. Let it flow through you in order to steward you to where you were meant to be."

LY **If there's one piece of advice you could give to a young WOC, what would it be?**

SL Just that you are both Sister and Goddess and so is every single woman of color you encounter. So please treat each other that way. We are way more powerful united than we will ever be divided.

LY **How can other women and sisters support one another when it comes to healing and expanding?**

SL Let go of everything that isn't love and keep showing up for one another. Keep holding space for each other's healing. Don't be afraid to unearth the darkness of our wounds so that we may bathe them in light. Learn how to build and maintain sacred, safe, and brave space for ourselves first and then our communities. Call on your ancestors for every damn thing, and remember you are forever protected by their prayers. Have and keep the faith. Our sisterhood will heal the world; after all, it is the most righteous act of revolution.

LY **I love your dress! What is the story behind it?**

SL Every time I travel to different countries in Africa, I love to check out local fashion designers (especially women designers). The dress I'm wearing is from a young designer from Zambia named Kapasa Musonda. You can find her unique designs on Instagram: @mangishidoll.

99

Chapter Four
The *V* Word

It is 8:15 A.M., and I hop out of my Lyft and walk through the iced-over snow and mud to enter the set for a photo shoot. There is always a woman greeting me. "Are you LaTonya?!" she asks. I answer yes. I arrive with my fro halfway twisted out and my face bare. At twenty-eight, my skin color is uneven and there is a patch of hormonal acne that I birthed along with Oak in the summer of 2014. "Clean face." When production sends out the call sheet for a shoot, this is what they often request. They check the color of my nails and the style of my hair, but the face part gets me the most.

This photo was taken by my dad during my first tennis lesson. I was nervous about wearing a dress and kind of refused to at first because I was self-conscious about my vitiligo. To make me feel better, my mom put makeup on my knees and face, and I felt so incredibly confident. The racket she got me was customized from Fingerhut, and I remember thinking, she put so much effort into this.

This is a routine I've executed many times over the past two years, as my blog and overall brand have grown, often creating an illusion of a glamorous life. The makeup artist comments on my cheekbones, and she adds shine to my eyelids and tint to my lips. And for a few hours, I forget about the girl with vitiligo. This is a far cry from the evenings I spent as a kid sobbing over the white patches that plagued my joints and my face. Vitiligo was not only something that altered the way I looked, but altered the way that I defined beauty.

Vitiligo is a medical condition that causes skin to turn white with the loss of melanocyte cells, which produce melanin. It is considered an autoimmune disorder (which can pair itself with another disorder soon after diagnosis or later in life), and it can arrive without reason. Some doctors and researchers believe that it is genetic; some believe it can be brought on by emotional distress. Vitiligo can be focal and localized, or it may affect several different areas on the body. The average age vitiligo appears in someone is twenty-five. *Twenty-five*. For me, it appeared in 1996. I was a seven-year-old, fifty-pound black girl turning white without warning or cause.

It all started when the corners of my mouth started to ache when I smiled. Initially, there were whispers, then adults would comment abrasively. Kids were dumb. Adults were assholes. Once I was in the checkout line at a Family Dollar store when a woman approached me and asked, "Awww, were you burned?" "No," I answered, half expecting the conversation to end there, but knowing that it never could. "Well, what is that?" *That*! Why did I need to explain something I hardly understood? One beautiful summer day, before the white started to move under my eyes, I sat in the backseat of my mother's car, refusing to step a foot out of it. The process was indescribably painful in varying degrees. "It just really hurts in the sun!" I cried, as our car drove into the sun's path. I felt the heat of the sun. I felt the sting of the vitiligo.

The ache around my mouth turned to ash, and the ash crawled its way to the sides of my mouth, forming a beard. It wasn't stark, but it was obvious to me and those near to me. Over the course of a few weeks, the ash started to peel away, exposing a white complexion, like a slab of meat coming off the bone. Soon after, the process began on my joints. Patches started to cover my knees, elbows, ankles, and eventually my knuckles. The faded speckles on my shin and foot proved that maybe the vitiligo wasn't as biased as I once had hoped. Sometimes, when I closed my eyes real tight, I imagined myself as a paper doll, full of color, with someone taking an eraser and diligently going to

This was taken after school during middle school
when I was doing homework at the kitchen table.
I'm wearing my layered Bazooka shirt and have
flat-ironed bangs. I used to bump them really big
and put my hair in a tight ponytail.

work on my body. First, they rubbed out my face, then they started on my knees and slowly moved to my ankles. At seven, I was being erased.

I was bullied, but I was a fighter. I'm not sure which came first. Two feet on the ground. Hip out. Fist tight. Cover the face. Wrap the hair around the right. Left hook. One September, when we lived in Long Island with my cousin, my uncle gave me a piece of fighting advice right before school began, anticipating the acclimation we were about to be presented with: "If they're big, hit them in the gut. The bigger they are, the harder they fall," he said, creating a stance and pointing to key spots on his body. I'm not sure if he was right, but my mind held on to that technique. My older brothers had spent years fighting, too. Maybe it was seeing how they needed to defend themselves that made throwing up my hands in pure animalistic survival mode a bit easier.

Once, at recess, I had a full-blown panic attack, knowing the bully in my class just *wanted* to fight me. "She's not going to let you ignore her. Before she comes to you, you should already have dirt in your hand to throw at her face so you can get the first hit," my friend said, in an attempt to protect my gangly body. The dirt worked. There was the set of twins in the lunchroom one morning at cafeteria breakfast, the girl in the playground, the boy that I was crushing on (and someone I called a friend), who sent a torn piece of paper with the drawing of a cow around class. "This is LaTonya. Hahaha," he wrote. And more.

My vitiligo was alive and visible but had become such a part of me that I subconsciously did things to hide it. If a stranger walked behind me, I'd naturally pose myself with crossed arms, so I wouldn't show the chunks of white on my elbows. When I needed to hold a pen, or have my hands and knuckles be the center of attention, I'd avoid it by simply interlocking my fingers and turning my hands inside out. Or I'd pretend my hands were cold (even in the heat of summer) and tuck the right one between my thighs, and my left hand under my left thigh. You would never see me willingly walk in front of anyone. I was too afraid they'd whisper about the white patches. I alternated between jeans and capris in the sweltering summer heat, and I either rolled up the sleeves of long-sleeved shirts or gravitated to three-quarter-length sleeves. I disliked every kid from ages four to eleven who was in the strange stage of life between not knowing better and knowing better, but would still loudly comment about my skin to their parents anyway.

This was taken the day I graduated high school.
When I moved back to New York, my mother and
grandmother sent me to a small Christian academy
in Brooklyn. I'm wearing a full face of MAC makeup,
and, for once, have semi-straight hair.

In 2006, my family moved back to New York to settle here for good. There is something about New York that allows you to be simultaneously invisible and visible. As a teenager returning to a big city when vitiligo was such a large part of my physical features, there was a part of me that needed that invisibility. But, equally, there was a part of me that craved to be visible in a healthier form. To be seen simply as a New York teenager, not a New York teenager *with* vitiligo. But I couldn't take on this city the way I needed to with my vitiligo being this thing that created a story *for* me. I had to do something.

We were with my grandmother in her Classon Avenue apartment when I finally opened up to my mother about my fear of living in Brooklyn with my vitiligo. Soon after, my mother took me downtown to Fulton Street, where a cluster of mom-and-pop stores blended with jewelry store after jewelry store run by men layered in gold necklaces and rings, hustling deals in front and passing out flyers. We dodged the guys with CDs on the street, and I heard Christian music blasting from the man at the fold-out table a block or so away from McDonald's. There was Conway (my grandmother's favorite), Cookie's, and Jimmy Jazz, too. My mom and I made our way into Macy's, passing through the bags, cornering around the cloud of perfume, and eventually stopping at the makeup counter. "This is what Angela uses," my mom said with confidence. Angela was one of my mom's best friends, who had vitiligo and lupus. I remember her as southern, frail, beautiful, incredibly warm, supportive, and frequently ill. She passed away a few years later. It wasn't just the vitiligo I feared; it was knowing that the vitiligo often led to lupus—sickness—an early mortality.

"You need two different shades. One for your knees and another for your face," the lady at the counter said. "Show her so she can do it herself," my mom requested. "Just blend," the lady chimed in as I applied it from my laugh lines to my cheekbones. I also needed a setting powder, so we bought it. And I needed brushes, so we bought those, too. I knew how to apply makeup already. Most mornings I'd perch myself on the toilet and watch as my mother readied herself for work. And so, my own routine of eye shadow, eyeliner, and Dermablend was something I did with ease. With the makeup, I assimilated to life as a young woman in Brooklyn quickly and naturally. Soon after Macy's, I started to straighten my hair, I rode the B52 bus from Bushwick through Bed-Stuy, and heard my grandmother

108

From the summer of 2009, wearing cut-off capris in McCarren Park in Brooklyn. Later that summer I got more comfortable with not covering up my vitiligo so much. But it took work. I would ride that cruiser everywhere, but I hardly wore a helmet because it would flatten out my bowl cut.

playfully say, like she always had whenever we found ourselves standing in her kitchen together, "Brooklyn girls. Best in the world!"

That afternoon at Macy's was something my mother and I both needed and loved. It was an intersection of my beauty and my pain, and the parts of it that she carried as my mother. The first few years after the vitiligo appeared, my mother had me experiment with diets the doctors said might help. Organic jams, soy milk, and alternative cereals—spelled out on a paper hung on the fridge. They also suggested that she change my environment; stress and trauma from our home had likely brought it on. The same doctors said that the vitiligo was likely not going to progress, but would stay the same or get better with care and a stress-free environment. They warned against the sun, so I became accustomed to wearing oversize sun hats and lathering with sunblock. In 2008, after a year or so in Brooklyn, I stopped using the layers of Dermablend and went straight to MAC, because my vitiligo had started to clear on its own. My MAC shimmer foundation blended best with the orange undertone of my skin. I used it as a spot treatment, only lightly covering the faded notes of vitiligo that remained on my face. And in the summer of 2010, I stopped covering my elbows and ankles with seasonally inappropriate clothes.

Occasionally, when I'm stressed for long periods of time, I get a glimpse of that seven-year-old girl in the form of a random white patch. She is standing right there looking at me. Having vitiligo as a kid created a version of beauty that is complicated and joyful. There is rarely a week that goes by that I don't remember the six-, seven-, or eight-year-old version of myself that is in pain. To be reminded of that level of trauma, while still being so incredibly thankful that the vitiligo has subsided, is to also be made aware of my own joy. My sensitivity to the physical "otherness" of strangers is something I can't erase. I don't want to.

The camera keeps clicking. I smile as wide as I naturally do, and I am told I was made for the camera. My skin shines. My face is photogenic. "You're a pro!" they say. Vitiligo is not something you talk about in between call sheets and bare-face requests. I don't think my seven-year-old self would have thought of such a thing.

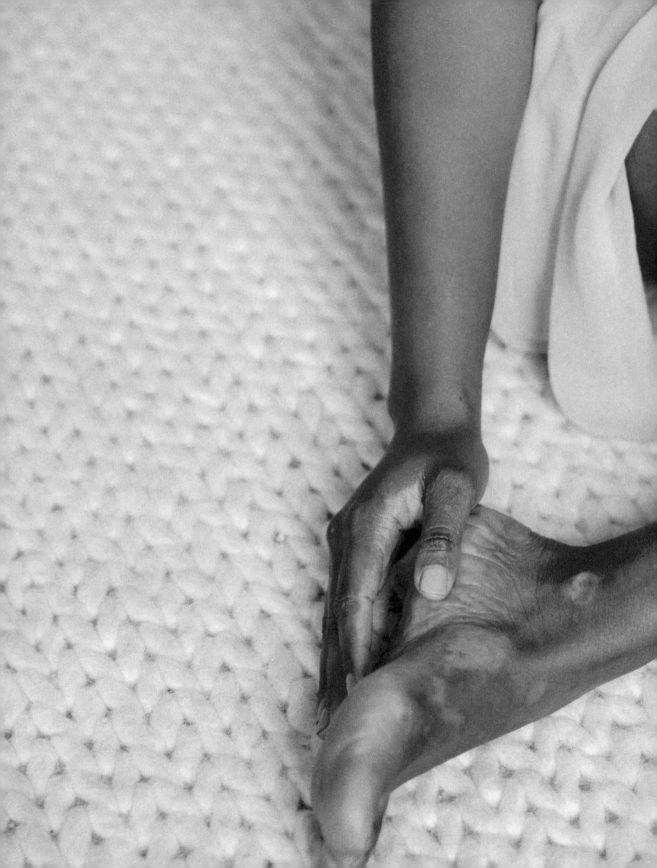

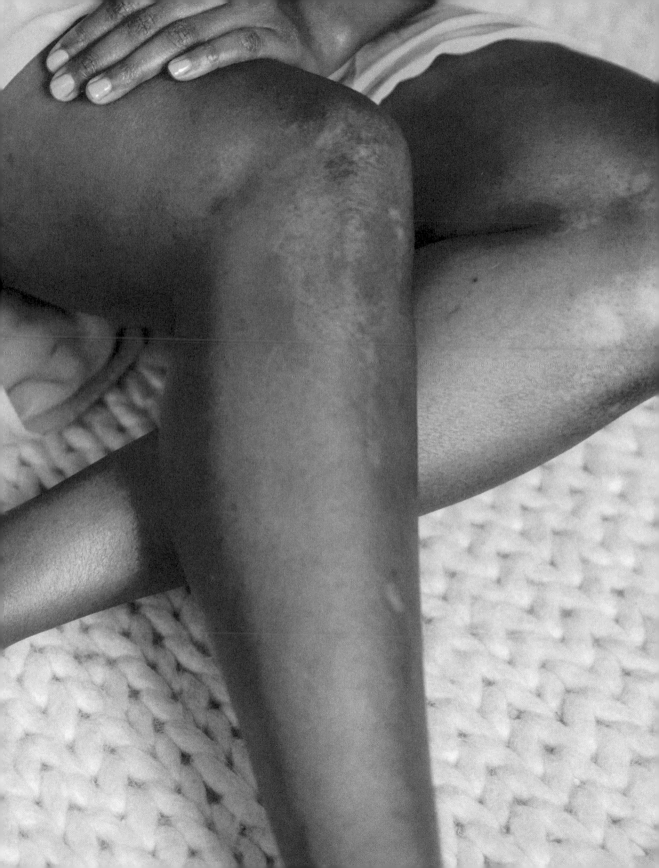

5 Rules for Supporting Your Child through Bullying

1. Get to know the parents and kids in your child's school. Make yourself as present as possible. Teachers, other parents, and your child are less willing to ignore inappropriate behavior when there is parental visibility.

2. Have in-depth, casual, and thoughtful conversations about school days and activities. Make them the core of recentering you and your child and what he/she may be going through at any given time.

3. Without pressure, reaffirm any physical and emotional boundaries, so that if there are boundaries crossed that seem particularly harmful, your child feels more inclined to discuss them.

4. Keep the opportunity open for conversations between your child and another adult without you. Sometimes kids don't tell parents things, but will tell another safe adult. Let the other adult know that they can reaffirm this relationship with your child without your presence, allowing conversations and trust to develop.

5. Clearly divide acceptable behavior and unacceptable behavior by bullies. The goal is to avoid having your child internalize the inappropriate and painful behavior of others.

How-to
Apply Morning Makeup in Two Minutes

My morning makeup routine has transitioned from being several minutes long to only two minutes. This has been partly because I apply less makeup than I used to, but also because I now have two children I have to get ready in the mornings. I feel most comfortable in my skin knowing its history. I feel most comfortable with the way I can bring out the natural features of my face with these few short steps.

1 **Cleanse.** I use CeraVe Hydrating Facial Cleanser, just water, or Thayers Witch Hazel to tone and refresh my skin. My face is naturally oily, and from years of having vitiligo, I've become used to not cleaning my face with various commercial products. While doctors didn't explicitly say that I shouldn't use products, the reversal of my vitiligo (combined with naturally acne-free skin) left me resistant to using anything that wasn't natural. If I do want a deeper clean, I skip the CeraVe and use a clean oil (like grapeseed or jojoba) with water.

2 **Moisturize.** Despite having more oily skin, I still moisturize after cleansing every morning and evening. I go between using a few drops of jojoba oil and CeraVe Facial Moisturizing Lotion (with SPF) or Drunk Elephant B-Hydra Intensive Hydration Gel.

3 **Conceal.** For under my eyes, I use Nars Radiant Creamy Concealer. I apply a few strokes, then blend with my finger going down.

  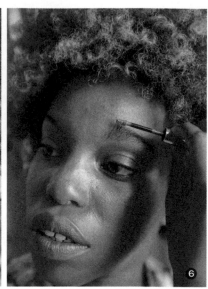

4 **Spot (Im)Perfection.** Oftentimes I don't mind, and then sometimes I do. When I want to cover the remaining vitiligo spots, or just even out my skin tone overall, I use MAC Mineralize Moisture with SPF. I just use a drop and apply where I feel is necessary. Normally, there are just two to three spots around my mouth.

5 **Glow.** In general, I like to look as natural as possible, and for me that means pumping up my natural shine and skin tone. To help with this, I use Fenty Beauty Match Stix Shimmer Skinstick in "Sinamon" for my cheekbones and eyelids.

6 **Brows and lashes.** I haven't waxed or plucked my eyebrows in about two years, so they're naturally a bit wild. To help with this, I use Glossier's Boy Brow to fill in my eyebrows a bit more and to help lay the stray hairs down.

I keep my eyelashes simple and go for the CoverGirl mascara I get at Target. I've used it since I was fifteen, and it has never failed me!

7 **Lips.** The color of my lips is close to the shade of my skin, so I either go natural or bold. Most days when I'm rushing out the door, I'll use a bit of Carmex and be on my way.

Anja Tyson

Brand Developer

I first met Anja through our mutual friend Scosha Woolridge. Scosha spoke so incredibly highly of her, I really couldn't wait to meet her. And when we did meet, we immediately clicked. Anja is a wordsmith, Saturday-brunch champion (and impeccable host), and a single mother to her four-year-old daughter, Matilda, among other titles. Whether our discussions are about motherhood, fashion, Brooklyn, relationships, racism, or being biracial, I come away still sizzling from them. Here is our conversation.

LY **What was your definition of beauty as a child?**

AT I loved old movies from the fifties and sixties when I was a kid, and I fell in love with Audrey Hepburn when I was nine or ten years old. I have definitely always been attracted to this sort of effortless, gamine version of beauty. I have never found loads of makeup very attractive. What's beautiful to me is as much about what is emanating from you as it is what you are wearing on your face. In retrospect, my beauty standards as a child were very white. When I first started wearing makeup recreationally, I was about twelve, and my mother bought me Cindy Crawford's new makeup book, *Basic Face*, which was basically this tutorial about everything you could want to know about wearing makeup in the year 1996. I remember turning to the page about face shapes and looking at the page, then looking in the mirror, then looking at the page again and realizing I didn't see anything in there that looked like me.

LY **As an adult, how have these definitions changed?**

AT I think that my beauty standards as an adult woman are much less self-loathing now. I am not comparing myself to blond supermodels with perfect skin these days, and I am much happier for it. But the basic tenet of what I believe is beautiful is still the same, and it's part of what I feel makes women so beautiful to begin with. I love clothing and dress and comportment and makeup and scent and all of these things . . . but I truly believe they are all accessories to your inner beauty, which is something everyone can see no matter what you cover it with. I love a beautiful, genuine smile, a woman holding her child, looks of surprise, the way women look when they are not posing for other people— even if they're just carrying groceries on the subway or getting out of a taxi or something. Confidence to live your life and be yourself and not hold back out of fear or concern for other people's opinions is the most beautiful—and probably also the sexiest—thing I can imagine. Whenever I catch myself being too self-conscious I try to take a breath, shake it out, and start again.

123

"Confidence to live your life and be yourself and not hold back out of fear or concern for other people's opinions is the most beautiful—and probably also the sexiest—thing I can imagine. Whenever I catch myself being too self-conscious I try to take a breath, shake it out, and start again."

LY   **Were you bullied as a kid? How did you channel that?**

AT   Relentlessly. I am biracial but extremely light-skinned, which was really difficult for kids to understand in the eighties and nineties. We forget how much the world has changed and opened up in the last few decades, but in 1994, when I was ten, I distinctly remember being asked by some kid if my orthodontia was what was "making my lips so big." And I was like . . . "No, it's because my dad is black." [*rolls eyes*]

I still have a lot of trust issues from being bullied so much as a child, both with new people and with people I am already very close to. It had a major impact on my self-esteem and confidence for a very long time. . . . But being bullied is also what gave me my drive, my competitive spirit, and my very, very close personal relationship with myself. I think there are a lot of things in each of our lives that we'd rather not have experienced, but for me this has become a part of my past that makes me indomitable for the future.

LY   **Are there any beauty rituals that speak to both the inner and outer versions of you?**

AT   My biggest and most time-consuming ritual is flat-ironing my hair weekly. I do it myself. I never go to a salon, and it's a very time-intensive process that means spending a lot of time with myself on a regularly recurring basis. I don't get a lot of "me time" in my life, so what used to be a tedious and tiresome ritual has turned into my self-care moment for each week, which has made me resent it much less. My hair has been through a lot, both physically and spiritually, and weekly I have to come to terms with that. And it means I can never get too far away from myself, because I have been battling with this hair since I was a little kid, and there it is . . . still sitting on top of my head, causing trouble, keeping me on my toes.

LY   **What are some lessons you hope Matilda learns in the day-to-day from you?**

AT   People talk about parenting like it's the SATs. Like you cram for it while you're pregnant and then when you give birth you have all the tools already and you just spend the rest of your life raising a human with those same tools. But in reality, it's more like the Hunger Games. There is literally no way to tell what's going to happen in either of your lives, and you don't stop developing as a person once you've had a kid. . . . Part of me hopes that Matilda skips all of the nonsense of feeling insecure or ugly that I went through. . . . She's a very cute kid, but beyond her looks she just emanates light. The way people react to her is amazing, and this all gives me so much hope that she will know from a much younger age than I did that her beauty starts within. And I think that will change the landscape of her experience as an awkward preteen or as a twenty-something girl making a ton of mistakes (there is no other kind of twenty-something girl). I don't know how much I have to teach her about beauty, but my hope is that I can be an attentive gardener to her spirit, and that as she grows and blossoms into herself through her whole life, I will be given the time and the presence to help her through those phases.

125

Chapter Five
Baldy Bean

In the fall of 2016, Solange released her third album, A Seat at the Table, not only as an artistic endeavor, but as a reclamation and proclamation of her roots. It was by a black woman for black women. With the album's release, Solange also revolutionized her style, becoming an undisputed fashion maven. There are pictures of her sitting in the studio, her hair back and a bit messy. Then there is the iconic image of her on the album, where colorful clips pin down soft, shoulder-length waves. In an interview with her sister, Beyoncé, Solange explained that the clips signified a transition, an anticipation of reaching the other side.

My mother took this when I was six months or so. Bald, in my walker, playing, looking, and likely observing. This photo reminds me so much of the pictures I have of River in her walker at our first apartment.

I knew this transition well, physically and emotionally. That same year, one sunny Saturday I was in our 650-square-foot DeKalb Avenue apartment, cleaning. The apartment smelled of lavender and palo santo, and "Don't Touch My Hair" started to slowly dip out of the speaker. River immediately ran out of her room into the living room, as if the song itself was an alarm. She was wearing too-short pajama pants that stopped right at her skinny shins, a fitted T-shirt that rose when she lifted her arms, and her hair was wild and big with loose curls. She jumped on our tufted green sofa and started singing and dancing along. She swung her hair, and the only words that sounded faintly similar to the lyrics happened to be those of the title. I stood in the middle of the living room, moving my own body, while wrapping the palms of my hands around my fro, so fully feeling Solange's words within. We were transported.

A few weeks later, I met Solange in a sardine-packed VIP zone in Bed-Stuy, where she bent low, whipped her hair around in circles, and found no shortage of surfaces to dance on. My friend Cleo had invited me out, and I threw on what I could find and jumped into a car on a rainy and warm Brooklyn evening. My own fro was tucked under an orange vintage woven hat with a wide brim that I had bought earlier that summer for $4. The room was hot, and save for Afropunk, I don't think I've been in a space that held such an enormous amount of joyful black girls with natural hair. My friend Piera and I danced, and eventually, Cleo pulled me past the narrow roped-off area to join her and Solange's friends. Yes, we were only dancing, but to dance with so much joy and conviction, and to have fros shape and shift and eventually fall limp with the humidity that overtook the room, moved my soul. At one point, Solange and I danced side by side, and she complimented my stoop-find hat and said she recognized me and my "beautiful babies." I didn't tell her that a few weeks earlier, my daughter, who had spent many days and weeks asking me to blow her curly hair bone-straight, had found comfort and confidence in Solange's record one afternoon in our tiny Brooklyn apartment.

* * *

Now and again, I can hear my father's voice call me "Baldy Bean" so distinctly. Baldy Bean was a nickname he came up with right after I was

Top My mom would try new braiding styles in my hair pretty often. This was the summer after my fifth-grade graduation, and I loved this style. She took this picture before she finished and put the ends in boiling water to seal them.

Above My mother and sister still do my hair to this day. Lately, my mother puts in box braids for my birthday and I keep them far beyond their expectancy. But when the city is hot and humid, and you're taking care of young kids and running around, there is no better hairstyle to get you through your days.

born, because I was the only one of his kids born without hair. In many of my baby photos, I am round with squinty eyes and a shiny bean of a head. There is a myth within the black community that says those who have very little hair when they are born usually have the thickest hair later in life. My hair didn't start growing in until I was about three. I was around five when it thickened and grew wild, and I heard my family's stories of my baldness and their predictions of my future hair's length while sitting at a dinner table or at a birthday party. On Sundays, I'd sit between my mother's legs on the cold hardwood floor as she styled it for the week. "Move more to the left," she would say while twisting my head. "LaTonya, head down!" as I would slowly creep my eyes up to catch a glimpse of the show we were watching. There were the seasons of combing, parting, doo-doo braids and bo-bos, hot combs (including the one time I reached over one and it burned my wrist), and eventually a perm.

The year I begged for a perm, I was eleven and we were living in Maryland. That was the year I was obsessed with *The Rugrats Movie* soundtrack, which included one of my favorite songs: "Take Me There" by Mya and Blackstreet, featuring Mase and Blinky Blink. The year before, in 1998, Mya sang the hook to Pras's song "Ghetto Supastar."

> *Ghetto supastar, that is what you are*
> *Comin' from afar, reachin' for the stars*

I kept my hair pulled up and tight, and the oversize puff that escaped my bo-bo floated above, making it easy to spot me from a distance. My aunts and cousins said that the song "Ghetto Supastar" was for me. For my hair. Something about my nature in combination with my hair—they'd sing "Ghetto supastar, that is what you are!" each time I entered a room. I was proud of my hair and the way its natural wildness differentiated me from others, but I still begged for the perm.

In the summer of 1999, right before my mom reluctantly leaned in to giving me the perm, I spent fifteen minutes in her bathroom with a dollar razor that I am sure she used for her legs. I saw how my sister, Brittany, secretly shaved her underarms and legs, and how my mother would tweeze her eyebrows, and then fill them in with a dark brown pencil every morning. Using a razor to just "clean" mine up felt like a girl's

Left Me and Oak on Mother's Day,
sitting in the Brooklyn Botanic
Garden after a day of riding bikes.

Right Shot on film by Peter after
a day of walking around Brooklyn,
summer 2009.

Clockwise from top

The summer Peter and I started dating, I had a bowl cut. I would sometimes part it on the side and gel it down, giving my hair a different look. Here, I wore my grandmother's clip-on earrings with the style.

I love having my hair braided in simple cornrows going straight back. It gives my hair a break, and the process is just as enjoyable now as it was when I was a kid.

This photo was taken on Christmas, a day or so after I went to get a wash and set at the Dominican salon. The signature look was a bit of a bump from large rollers. I can still tell when someone has just had a wash and set, and I suppose many NYC women of color can, too.

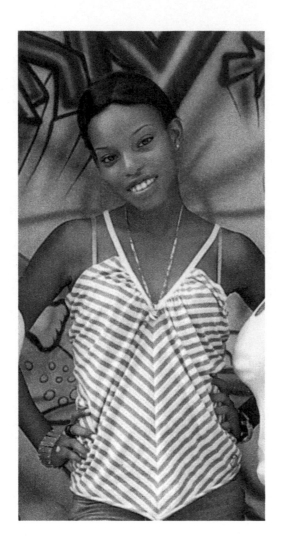

134

The West Indian Day Parade is a big deal in Brooklyn. I got a wash and set the day before and wore a fresh doobie wrap to the parade. I had to go to work right after, so I took the wrap out once I got to Skechers.

passage into womanhood. I think it was there that I first encountered a requirement for growing up as a girl, as I was faced with a choice between settling into the hair I was given or ridding myself of it. I placed the pink razor in my hand and gently inched my way up to my right eyebrow. Just a little clean, I said. My hand slipped. Striking one fat gap in my right eyebrow. For the rest of the summer, my three brothers would taunt me with a rap lyric from Jay-Z's "Do It Again" featuring Amil and Beanie Sigel: "Three cuts in your eyebrows tryna wild out." The year 1999 was what I'd like to call the most ridiculous meld of lyrics and hair.

Before getting my own hair permed, I watched the white cream of Just for Me settle into my sister, Brittany's, hair, transitioning it within minutes folded into methodical steps. It made her already soft-textured hair a bit softer, and the curls at her roots almost flat to the scalp. When it was my turn, my hair took the perm, but not well. It was never straight enough or long enough. The cream burned my scalp and left thick and flaky scabs no matter how much Vaseline laced my head. At the first sign of moisture in the air, my roots would start forming waves and the ends would thicken with a humidity puff. Black girl perm code: Don't touch your hair! But what girl doesn't fix her hair when it seems to want to return itself to an annoying wildness only saved for the salon on Saturdays?

The women in my family set aside 9 A.M. to 1 P.M. every other Saturday for a visit to the local Dominican salon for a wash, roller set, and then a doobie wrap. I don't know how old I was when I got my first doobie wrap, but I remember being so incredibly excited for it. I would get the chance to see how long my hair really was—it was something in their conditioner, or in the way they set their rollers, or how they blew it out. Dominican women who propped shop and opened early mornings and closed late had this power within the black community. While I loved the Dominican salon, it was the first time I smelled the pungent clash between Latin people of color and black people. Whether in the salon or from a family member, I heard I had "good hair." "Good hair" seemed to falsely offer clarity in race and culture blends. I felt the need for that distinction, too.

For years, I had embarrassingly gone back and forth between claiming my Panamanian roots and completely ignoring them. There were evenings I spent dancing bachata and merengue in Washington Heights

with the Dominican friends I met when I worked at Skechers. There were the times I wore a Panamanian flag at the West Indian Day Parade on Eastern Parkway. And there were the many moments in between, when I was asked my origins and I only claimed that my parents were simply black and from Brooklyn. My grandmother was half indigenous American, and I had spent part of my childhood at her dad's house after school with uncles and cousins, but I only claimed that part of me when it felt necessary. It all depended on if I was hanging out with my Puerto Rican friends, my Dominican friends, or my black or white friends (who essentially identified Panamanians as black). The lines were blurred.

Right before my grandmother's death, I went to the Butterfly Dominican salon on Nostrand Avenue and dyed my hair a golden brown to match hers. I went every week after visiting her, cutting inch by inch, until I was left with a bowl cut. I still went after she died, peeking around the corner to see if there was anyone new on the block, if much had shifted on her street since she left. Three days before I found out I was pregnant, I got the sides of my hair shaved off. When River was just a few months old, I strapped her to my chest in the BabyBjörn as my stylist clipped my ends. And a few days before I got married, I went to refresh my golden dye and left with a cranberry reddish tint (a complete fail).

River was eighteen months old when we lived in Bushwick and I found this hole-in-the-wall Dominican salon a half block away from the grocery store where I spent many late evenings arguing with the manager about honoring my WIC checks. The salon had a store in the back, and they complimented me on the way my hair was cut but shamed me on its texture. "Please cut it all off," I asked one evening, after stumbling in kidless. I had spent a few weeks letting my perm grow out so that my natural hair would have time to reveal itself. The next morning, after listening to Otis Redding, I sat in front of my computer and took an obscene amount of Photo Booth pictures during River's nap. I wasn't bald, but I was close. I felt beautiful. I felt free.

5 rules for Caring for Your Natural Hair

1. Don't be afraid to start again. When I cut my hair, everyone was taken aback by my choice in transition, but I realized that I was able to truly feel the effects of that transition by cutting it all the way off. If in the process of being natural you need to start again (again), don't be afraid to just cut it off. I think the evolving identity around natural hair is one in which fluidity is a core element.

2. All hair (and products) are not created equal. When I first started styling my natural hair, I would watch all of the YouTube videos of girls with different kinds of hair styling with several products. When I would try, I never received the same result. Working with products and hair is often trial and error, and your hair texture, cut, and ability to adapt to products is your own. Be patient.

3. Use heat-safe products when blow-drying or ironing your hair, but don't let others' opinions on heat keep you from using it. Whether it is dye or heat, there seems to be a need to define how natural is natural among naturalists. Again, no one can define this for you. Do what's best for you and your hair.

4. Your hair is what you eat. Want longer, hydrated, and fuller hair? Then eat like it. What we ingest comes back out. Whenever I haven't had enough water over the course of a few days, I can see it in my hair.

5. Create boundaries around your hair and how you style and talk about it. I realized that while I didn't have an immediate reaction to a friend or someone touching my hair or asking me questions, eventually it all became too much and I was angry and annoyed. Your hair is part of your body, and while everyone should be aware and knowledgeable on what to do and not to do, it doesn't hurt to articulate your boundaries as you rock your crown!

How-to Tie a Head Wrap

I use head wraps in between styling weeks, when I'm feeling a bit lazy, or as a simple way to add color and texture to my outfit. I love golds, light blues, pinks, and reds on my skin. They are colors that don't wash me out or distract from my face, but pump up my overall look. For a full look, a head wrap fabric should at least be 62 by 17 inches (157.5 by 43 cm), or you can shop for one at a head wrap–specific shop. The ones I usually wear are neck scarves by Block Shop Textiles. The prints are made in India, and the fabrics are light. The scarves hold up well with weather, washing, oil, and whatever else your hair has to withstand. In short, wraps are just another way for style and creativity to meet.

1 Wrap the fabric below your crown from the back of your head. You want to make sure you have an even amount of fabric in your left and right hands.

Tip: If you're worried about your hair breaking, wear a silk scarf or bonnet under your wrap if it isn't silk.

2 Cross the fabric over at the center front of your head.

3 Pull that fabric back, cross it again below the crown in the back, and bring it to the front. (You should have two small pieces of fabric remaining in your left hand and right hand.)

4 Tie those two small pieces together, and then tuck the ends under a lip of fabric on each side of your head in the front.

5 There will be excess fabric at the back of your head under your crown. Take that fabric and pull it up and over the exposed hair, then tuck the fabric under the area where the other fabric was previously tucked.

6 Tuck in any hair hanging over your forehead, and voilà!

Julee Wilson

Fashion and **Beauty** Director, *Essence*

I first met Julee back in her *Huffington Post* days, when she was writing a story about motherhood and style. We were pregnant with boys at the exact same time and eventually had them just weeks apart. Over the years, as she has transitioned from the *Huffington Post* to *Essence*, our relationship has grown alongside our babies. Of equal importance, anytime I am "the black girl" at a mom-centric event, I can count on Julee to be there, too, with her bouncing hair and signature leg pump. I immediately feel at ease and can be the LaTonya who is often found running with a group of girlfriends in Brooklyn. With just a call across the room—"Heeyyy, Julee!"— the space's energy can change into what I can only describe as black-girl dopeness. Here is our conversation.

LY   **What was your relationship to your hair as a child?**

JW   From what I can remember, it was great. I honestly don't recall ever hating my hair—which I attribute to my parents teaching me to embrace every aspect of myself. Even so, growing up in predominantly white communities, there were moments where I wanted to emulate the silky, blows-in-the-wind manes of my white girlfriends. I remember tying long ribbons to the ends of my ponytails in order to re-create the length and movement. But ultimately those make-believe times were fleeting, and my adoration for my own beauty always prevailed. One of my fondest memories growing up is my dad straightening my hair with a stove-heated hot comb. He grew up in North Carolina with three sisters he helped raise, so he knows a thing or two about keeping a black girl's hair together. That love for me and the time we spent together while he pressed my tresses is priceless.

LY   **What's your relationship with your hair like now as an adult?**

JW   I absolutely love my hair. It's an extension of me. Black women are blessed with the most magical hair on earth. It can literally do anything—which is why I love experimenting with shapes and styles. One minute we can be rocking a fierce Afro, and the next we'll have a seriously smooth blowout. And then there are braids, and locs, and twists—oh my! Long story short, my love for my hair is limitless.

LY   **When did you go natural?**

JW   I've actually been natural most of my life. There was a time from ages twelve to fourteen that I relaxed my hair, because I thought it would make it more manageable. But my edges started breaking and my hair became so unhealthy. That's when I went completely natural and would heat-straighten my hair (i.e., my dad's hot combing).

151

"Black women are blessed with the most magical hair on earth. It can literally do anything."

LY **As a mother, what are some lessons you hope Orion learns from you?**

JW I think my lessons will be more about making sure I speak about myself in a positive manner. I want him to know that I love what I see in the mirror—in hopes that he will feel the same about himself. I obviously tell him that he is smart and handsome, but actions speak louder than words.

LY **When you care for your hair, what does that mean to you?**

JW It's truly an act of self-care. Sure, vanity is an aspect, but for the most part taking the time to love and nurture my crown is part of my wellness routine. Although it's not always easy to find the time between work, mothering, and wife-ing, it's a necessity. I also love the sense of community that black women create around our hair. I love the wisdom and love that it is exchanged, whether we're trying to figure out the best twist-out method or just praising each other's hairstyles on a particular day. Our bond is so beautiful.

LY **Has your hair shaped any of your experiences as a woman in your field?**

JW Definitely. Being a fashion and beauty director makes my hair not only an important aspect of my work (there are a lot of products I need to road test), but also my favorite accessory. We all know being a black woman is dope, and it's even doper that we can celebrate that beauty. And that's exactly what I do when I proudly rock my Afro! And thankfully I have a profession that appreciates that. My heart goes out to my sisters who feel like they can't fully express themselves with their hair because of their work environments.

153

Chapter Six

Birthing a Body, Growing a Woman

I gave birth to River in the middle of a New York City snowstorm during the winter of 2011. I wore a polyester leopard bandana around my head that pushed the finger-curled weave away from my face. My sister, Brittany, had sewn it in so that I could transition into motherhood without the worry of my hair. The Pitocin slowly dripped into my bloodstained right arm as I watched the snow fall from the third-floor hospital room that overlooked the East River.

A Polaroid of me and River by Peter,
from the day we told people about
the second pregnancy.

The strong vein in my left arm had given up after being improperly poked one too many times by a twenty-something nurse who mentioned "C-section" casually at 3 A.M. when River's heart rate dropped. The cord was wrapped around her neck; the epidural made me itchy; and I spent seven hours staring at the fetal heart monitor as her heart rate spiked and fell. Brittany trucked through the storm at 9 A.M. and whipped her pink shimmer lip gloss out of her purse and applied it to my cracked lips as I was getting ready to push. I complained of the pungent smell of blood and shit. Our birth plan said I would push and then they would lay my baby on my chest. I'd nurse her and we'd instantly connect.

I like to say that a new version of me was born when I birthed River, but I think the first transformation happened soon after I decided to keep her, late one evening after finally getting through to the abortion clinic. The procedure was going to cost too much. It would hurt too much. I was too late and too broke. Peter offered support: "I won't leave you." His parents offered what they could financially: "We will help you both take care of it if you choose this," they said on a three-way phone call. My mother offered reality: "Will you be able to do this alone, if all of this falls through?"

When we first announced we were keeping our baby, my father-in-law said, "Life happens when you're busy making plans." He was right. I hadn't known I was pregnant until I was too far along. My breasts ached and I went from 110 pounds to 117 pounds without reason. I got my first period early, at eleven; it stopped, and didn't come back until I was thirteen, so naturally, I didn't pay notice to the missed beat in my body's rhythm for a couple of months. But once I officially found out, other surefire signs of pregnancy revealed themselves. There were the migraines, and the pelvic aches, the uptick in my libido, and then, persistent nausea that made the simple so difficult. I often found myself scouting anything that smelled of ginger just to settle it momentarily. My routine of driving my pink cruiser from Clinton Hill through Bed-Stuy to Williamsburg was substituted for train rides that required I hop off and vomit on the part of the platform where the trash can furthest to the left meets the Spring Street sign. I packed peanut butter and jelly sandwiches for lunch almost every single day and ordered pierogis, cabbage, and mashed potatoes (heavy on the salt) on Saturdays. I had an aversion to pizza and coffee, and I could smell the stench of Woodhull Hospital (which was four blocks away from the house where we moved in Bushwick) as soon as I stepped out the front door.

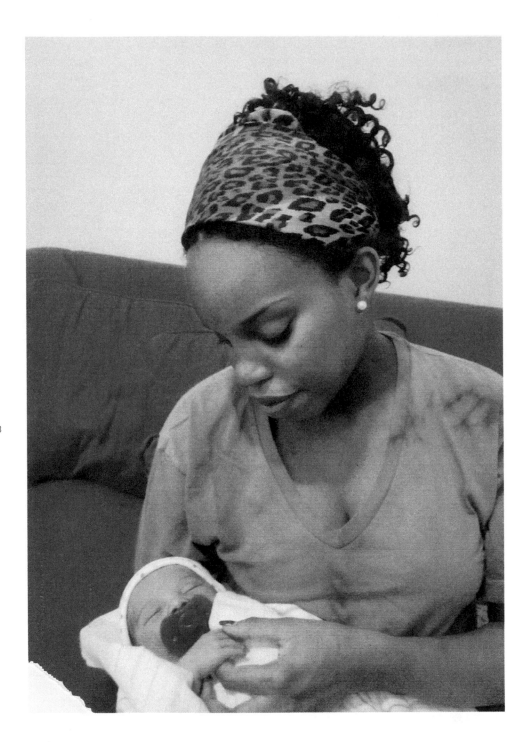

Me and River on the first day we got
home from the hospital.

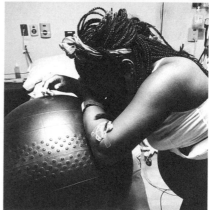

Clockwise from top right

I was two weeks overdue with Oak, and the last few days of my pregnancy were spent resting in our Brooklyn apartment in this Sonnet James dress that was the perfect mix of comfort and stretch.

Peter took this right before I gave birth to Oak. I had a thirty-six-hour unmedicated labor, and during the last stretch I was standing up and taking interval naps on that ball in the hospital.

Oak a few days after we brought him home from the hospital. This was his birth announcement photo.

During my pregnancy with River, my breasts tripled in size, and my nipples got two shades darker. Stretch marks crawled through my inner thighs. I used a rubber band to close Peter's jeans that I wore. For my hospital bag, my sister bought me pink Victoria's Secret sweatpants and a matching T-shirt. The sweatpants were tight around my butt, securing the size 8 Fruit of the Loom panties and overnight pads I wore as I walked around the house. The legs of the pants flared a bit at the ankle, so it didn't fully feel like I was conforming to sweats. The shirt was soft and allowed me to lift it and breastfeed River with ease. It hugged my postpartum belly in a way that provided that unique comfort a new mother craves once her body has transitioned. Seven years later and my body isn't nearly the same, but I still wear that outfit around my home.

"Hold on. Don't push!" Dr. N demanded as she tried to untangle the cord from around River's neck. "I can't stop!" I yelled back between breaths, raising my knees to my cheeks. My need to push caused me to tear, resulting in stitches. I sat on a clear inflated plastic donut for three weeks, and waddled to the dollar store around the corner from our tenement apartment as a field trip for exercise. When the waddling and pain from the tear subsided, but my jeans still didn't fit, I signed up for a membership at Lucille Roberts. At the gym, I felt the slab of skin between my vagina and butt slowly ripple apart under my black leggings as I used the abductor muscle. I lost most of the fifty pounds I had gained, but still sported a four-month postpartum pouch.

Learning my way around a new body shape, full of curves and stretch marks, was on par with what I had to map out within myself. One night, Peter dropped me off at my mom's house, and I felt what I can only describe as this intense longing to return home, kidless. Home wasn't this physical place. It wasn't my mom's house on Greene Avenue, and it wasn't even our home on Wilson Avenue. It wasn't New York. It had no form. And while it felt like something I knew, it was indistinguishable. I felt like a kid searching for familiar corners to hide in, but I was trapped in this field of new motherhood. It was wide open and raw, holding this six-pound baby they said belonged to me. I loved River so deeply from the start, and I knew what to do, but love, knowledge, and capabilities don't always align with a deep disconnection of self.

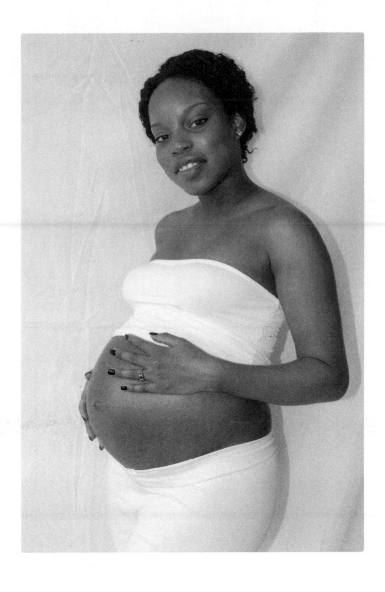

Right before I had River, we set up a simple backdrop, a camera, and a tripod and took our own pregnancy photos in our bedroom. I remember feeling the weight of River so heavy under my belly button, and feeling as if my stomach couldn't possibly make another inch of room for her.

162

On my babymoon at our friends' house in
Florida. I remember feeling so relieved that I
made it that far. That my belly was that round
and that we would be returning home and
could truly prepare for the baby.

When River was two, I got pregnant again. At nineteen weeks, I returned to New York from a work trip to California; the turbulence on the flight was so bad, I started to vomit over my sleeping toddler. Peter caught what he could with a plastic bag, and a stranger passed me some gum. I had peed on myself a little and there was blood, too. The flight was the start of yet another transformation. It is hard to map the sequence of events that led me to the hospital in Washington Heights, where the monitor was silent— no heartbeat—the baby had died. I was twenty-one weeks by then. Earlier, Dr. N had suggested an abortion. "The baby looks healthy, but there's so little amniotic fluid and we don't know why. It can't survive without it," she said. But I refused. She sent me to another specialist, who didn't know why my amniotic fluid had disappeared to only about a half of an inch. Then one night, I went to the emergency room, where I was again swabbed for leaking fluid. Of course, the swab returned negative.

In between visits that produced few answers but the same result— "You should have an abortion"—I joined a private premature-rupture group on Facebook. I received all of my answers from women who spent their days receiving no answers from their doctors or bodies. I nervously posted my story one evening, and almost instantly, the post received answers from anonymous women all over the world. They pointed me in the direction of similar stories, and reassured me of the likelihood that I did in fact have a small hole in my sac. Once after returning from yet another negative swab, I messaged with a woman from the group, to which she replied, "Of course it will be negative!" This run was normal for the group, and results were always a roll of the dice, and almost always, still, leaving few answers. The woman suggested cranberry juice to combat a possible infection, which a hole in my amniotic sac meant I was susceptible to, and with the tips from this group of women, sisters, and new friends, I drank cranberry juice, and spent two weeks on self-imposed bed rest, watching my two-year-old live a life without me and contemplating my own mortality. But there was still so much I had yet to learn.

After losing a baby, no one tells you that you will need to dig up that sports bra you wore while testing your abductor, and wear it again for weeks to stop the shriek of pain in your engorged breasts. They won't say that the sports bra will turn lavender because of the frozen cabbage leaves you stuffed in it to relieve the pain. When they admit you for the D & E,

163

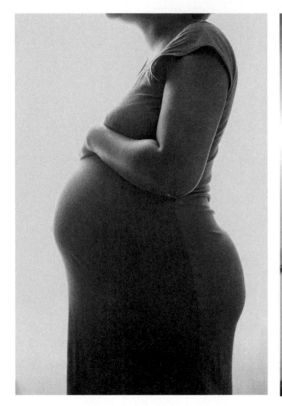

Left Eight or so months pregnant with
Oak. I documented the pregnancy with
a series that photographed both River
and my belly separately as we grew
week by week. It felt like a natural
extension, instead of focusing so much
on the pregnancy, which felt scary.

Right From a family vacation in
Florida, watching the sunrise with Oak.

they'll tell you it's the easy route, as your uterus contracts in a busy waiting room to try to naturally deliver the baby it holds within; they won't tell you that for the rest of your life, while sitting at any doctor's office, you'll have to—for a second—relive the large belly, the single track of fluorescent hospital lights floating above you as you were rolled in, or the way your daughter pressed your doughy belly and asked where the baby had gone. No one will tell you that there will be months relearning your body again and its functions, with the weight of loss written all over you, while having it deeply etched in the corners of your being.

I had another baby—quickly—and gained another fifty pounds. I had a thirty-six-hour unmedicated labor in our sublevel apartment on Clinton Avenue, and I reached down to pull my son out of my vagina at Methodist Hospital on Fifth. Unmedicated, because I wanted to watch what my body could do. I wanted to see to what degree I was or could be in control of my body. My therapist once pointed out that I control things by necessary means only. I manage chaos, and try to grab hold of things that feel as though they can slip into a space that is not only uncomfortable, but that will somehow create a further slip into a state of trauma. Trauma that doesn't encompass the joy I try to live within daily.

It was around 5 A.M. when I was rolled out of my delivery room holding an eight-pound Oak and shaking from the high that was his birth. I smiled at the tiny nurse who had wrapped a bedsheet around my waist, told me to drop my weight, and twisted my 180-pound body to get his head down through my vaginal canal. I thanked her, and she and all the other nurses watched me move through the hallway and affirmed that it was *me* who had done all the work. Less than forty-eight hours later I put him in a gold silk ring sling and walked him around our neighborhood, smiling and ridiculously content.

I have realized that birthing him wasn't truly about control. It was about power. Finally, birthing what belonged to me. What belongs to all women. This road is about pain, it is about pushing past limits, it is about joy, it is about becoming. All in all, growing is a process.

165

5 Rules for Accepting and Loving a Growing Body

1. Start slow. All too often we jump into these grand ideas of overwhelmingly loving ourselves, and end up not truly and deeply doing it.

2. Create a circle of friends who authentically share not only their own version of beauty, but also their flaws. Discuss this openly with them. Soon you'll realize that many women feel surface shortcomings. When you dive deeper, you allow yourself and other women the space to not only love yourselves more, but also question and critique the systems that divide our bodies from our versions of beauty and ultimate healing within our bodies.

3. Admire and celebrate other women. Silence breeds comparison. When we allow ourselves to praise others, we allow ourselves to heal.

4. Reevaluate what you consider flaws. Make a list of all the work your body has done. Seven is a good start. And each day for a week, thank your body for doing that work. Repeat.

5. Stare in the mirror at your reflection; touch what you love and hug what you don't. Sometimes we need to just love and mother ourselves.

Latham Thomas

Doula and Founder of Mama Glow

I met Latham at a Bugaboo event that I attended with River. Her son, Fulano, was DJ-ing and I was big with my second pregnancy. That afternoon, the aura that surrounded her was sweet and nurturing. It is no surprise that her work is grounded in ultimate self-care and sisterhood. From books to a new women's space in Williamsburg, Brooklyn, Latham's body of work is about one word: healing. I watched her as she moved around the room, and I think at one moment or another she congratulated me on my pregnancy. A few weeks later, I flew off for a work trip and subsequently lost the baby. Since then, we've attended and supported one another through a plethora of celebrations (and rainbow-baby pregnancy). Here is our conversation.

LY **As a mother, what has been your relationship to your body, and has there been a difference before birthing Fulano, during, and now, many years after?**

LT My relationship to my body is one of integration. I see my body as my partner and I defer to my body. I seek and heed its wisdom. All of the choices I make, I clear with my body first. The body speaks in clear and certain terms, through sensations, telling us what it needs and giving us information that we can use to respond and support ourselves in a way that honors the body. So when I am tired, I sleep. When I am hungry, I eat. When I get a nervous feeling about something, I don't do it. This is really the core of my self-care practice: a deep listening to the body. I wasn't always like this. When I was in my twenties, I pushed myself a lot more. I briefly bought into the hustle mentality, but I quickly realized that it was misaligned with who I am at my core, and I pushed back against that and surrendered to my self-care practice to fortify me. That's what helped me become embodied. When my son was born, I awakened to a new power rooted in my body and I have since learned to harness and use that power to advance myself and other women who are ready to return home to themselves.

LY **What is the connection between body and mind that you see?**

LT From my vantage point, the only lens to true understanding of the intricate processes that govern us is to honor that the mind and body are woven together. They support each other, and when we sever the connection we experience disease. . . . We have to reclaim our bodies as sacred, and that means doing the work to unshackle ourselves from the messages we have been told about our bodies.

LY **As a black woman, are there any obvious ways you feel like a black woman's body is often policed?**

LT Yes . . . it's interesting because the black body has always been commodified. When our ancestors were forcefully taken and brought to the Americas, they did backbreaking labor to build the foundations of those countries. In the US, our maternal ancestors wet-nursed the masters' babies and oftentimes did not even get to feed their own children. Our hairstyles and features—like high cheekbones, thick hips, and broad lips—are ever popular when someone else "puts them on," but certainly not when we naturally embody them. Our bodies are often hypersexualized. We never really stop to address how much we are actually carrying, how much ancestral pain, how much angst—where does that live in our bodies? We never have permission to express it. Our pain, sorrow, anxiety. We don't have outlets. And we are expected to contain ourselves and hold ourselves hostage in our own pain. This is why my work is about women reclaiming well-being and learning to mother themselves first.

171

"Joy is your birthright. And anything that keeps you away from your joy is binding you from freedom."

LY **How do you make your body feel good on a daily basis?**

LT Self-care is part of my gospel. It's what I preach about all the time. I call it "glow time." I'm about cultivating rituals and reveling in radical self-care. Slowing down to celebrate and love yourself, whether that's a hot bath, a foot rub, a full-body massage, taking a hike, or simply logging off of social media and reading a book. The moments we spend on ourselves and by ourselves are magical. I make space for glow time at various parts of the day. In the morning, I aim to rise up early around 5:30 or 6 A.M. and take my time to get ready. I sit on the roof and feel the fresh air. I move slowly, have a meditation moment, a little prayer. During the day, I might unfold my yoga mat and stretch it out at our women's space between clients, get a manicure and ten-minute massage, then get back to work. But nothing beats a hot bath in my Mama Glow bath soak.

LY **As a doula, what part of the transition into motherhood surprises you the most?**

LT I wouldn't use the word *surprise* but the word *awe*, which means wonder and reverence. I am in constant reverence of the mother. Even after witnessing hundreds of women at their most powerful and most vulnerable, it always feels like the first time. That's probably what's most surprising, is that it always feels like it's the first birth. It's magical. I love witnessing women transform into the most powerful version of themselves through the birth process. I love holding and gazing at the new infants and watching them grow. I'm an extended family member and love that the birth process forever bonds me with these families. One of the best parts about being a doula is watching women cross the threshold into motherhood. . . . I am inspired to make a difference each day, to touch someone in an impactful way.

This is why I am so compelled to do the work I do with women and mothers—ushering new life into the world requires a reverence for spirit and a celebration of the magic of the female body. The root of spirit is that it is in everything, everywhere; we are alchemists.

LY **Is there one piece of advice, specifically for women of color, that you wish someone had told you?**

LT Joy is your birthright. And anything that keeps you away from your joy is binding you from freedom. My advice is to let it go. Don't pack more than you can carry. So many of us are walking around carrying the baggage of our mothers and grandmothers. We don't have to carry their stuff. You don't have to walk through life carrying ancestral baggage. You can choose to repattern your life. Change the legacy so your children can be free of the burden of your pain. You can choose joy. It's yours. When you access emotional freedom, you can soar. We are deeply connected to everything around us, so really access your relationships and make sure the people that you keep close can really soar alongside you.

173

LY **Anything else you'd like to add?**

LT Anything we create takes patience, faith, and an ideal environment for growth. Be careful and gentle with what seeds you plant in the soil of your soul.

Just a few of my favorite *Brooklyn spots*

While much of my life has been spent flowing in and out of New York, for the past eleven years, I've been here choosing to plant roots in the cement. I had both of my children near the place I was born. Many of their "firsts" have been near mine, or my mother's, or someone in my family's. Many of the people are gone; the buildings and apartments, no longer: just cascades and new faces and people with a very faint grasp on the history here. Why I choose to live here. Why I choose to change and grow, not as a woman of color, but as a woman of color raising a family. Still, Brooklyn and the memories I've been privileged enough to make in it despite its rapid change are not lost on me. These are just a few of my favorite places, and so many of the memories that they hold are near and dear to my heart.

Eat

Ample Hills Creamery

623 Vanderbilt Avenue
Brooklyn, NY 11238

Bittersweet

180 DeKalb Avenue
Brooklyn, NY 11205

Brooklyn Crab

24 Reed Street
Brooklyn, NY 11231

Eugene & Company

397 Tompkins Avenue
Brooklyn, NY 11221

Peaches HotHouse

415 Tompkins Avenue
Brooklyn, NY 11216

Sweet Chick

164 Bedford Avenue
Brooklyn, NY 11211

Urban Vintage

294 Grand Avenue
Brooklyn, NY 11238

Mosey

Brooklyn Botanic Garden

900 Washington Avenue
Brooklyn, NY 11225

Brooklyn Bridge Park

334 Furman Street
Brooklyn, NY 11201

Brooklyn Central Library at Grand Army Plaza

10 Grand Army Plaza
Brooklyn, NY 11238

Brooklyn Museum

200 Eastern Parkway
Brooklyn, NY 11238

Fort Greene Park and Greenmarket

DeKalb Avenue
Brooklyn, NY 11201

Museum of Contemporary African Diasporan Arts (MoCADA)

80 Hanson Place
Brooklyn, NY 11217

Prospect Park

Brooklyn, NY 11225

Play

Brooklyn Academy of Music

30 Lafayette Avenue
Brooklyn, NY 11217

Cobble Hill Park

Clinton Street
Brooklyn, NY 11201

Jane's Carousel

Old Dock Street
Brooklyn, NY 11201

McCarren Park Pool

776 Lorimer Street
Brooklyn, NY 11222

New York Transit Museum

99 Schermerhorn Street
Brooklyn, NY 11201

Underhill Playground

117B Underhill Avenue
Brooklyn, NY 11238

Underwood Park

Lafayette Avenue
Brooklyn, NY 11205

Dance

Baby's All Right

146 Broadway
Brooklyn, NY 11211

Lovers Rock

419 Tompkins Avenue
Brooklyn, NY 11216

Friends and Lovers

641 Classon Avenue
Brooklyn, NY 11238

Ode to Babel

772 Dean Street
Brooklyn, NY 11238

183

Shop

Brooklyn Charm

145 Bedford Avenue
Brooklyn, NY 11211

Brooklyn Flea

80 Pearl Street
Brooklyn, NY 11201

Feliz

185 DeKalb Avenue
Brooklyn, NY 11205

L Train Vintage

654 Sackett Street
Brooklyn, NY 11217

Martine's Dream

681 Nostrand Avenue
Brooklyn, NY 11216

Scosha

64 Grand Street
Brooklyn, NY 11249

Acknowledgments

This book could not have been written without the help and love of so many. First, River, thank you for pushing me to dream bigger and for being the true marker for the way in which love can expand outside oneself. Oak, thank you for teaching me to slow down and love stronger: my body, my children, those around us. You both are complete joys each and every day. There has been no bigger lesson than in being your mom. I love you both so much.

Peter, thank you for the last near-decade journey. And, of course, for the two most beautiful and loving things that this life could ever offer. Mommy, there aren't enough pages or words for you. Thank you for all that you've done for me and for all of us. My brothers and sister, who share some of these stories but on their own, in their own lens: without you, life would be a complete bore. My grandmother, aunts and uncles, nieces and nephews, I LOVE YOU in this world and beyond.

Annette and Charles, thank you for your love and support from the very start. I love you.

There were so many hands that went into this project. There were so many people and places that cared for me while I worked on this. Christian, thank you for your friendship and tremendous support, from the late-night calls and first round of edits to helping me see how far language could move beyond me. This book wouldn't be what it is without you. Thank you, Dr. Rose, for the sessions. Thank you, Nakita, Shi Shi, and Adam for your limitless care and love for River and Oak during the many afternoons, late nights, and early mornings. You all made them both feel like everything was more than all right, all the time.

To Max, for going so hard for me all the time, THANK YOU. To Alison, Sarah M., Deb, Heesang, and the entire Abrams team for believing in me and this project. Georgia, thank you for planting the seed that one summer. Bee, Rubi, Nicole, Laramie, Josie, Hannah, Anja, Aurora, Sade, Julee, and Latham, thank you for the week of women magic and creativity. It was such a time.

Karyn, thank you for passing down the magic apartment in which this project was written, and in which my son was nursed back to health. A special thank-you to Dr. Langstner, Dr. Mosca, and the amazing nurses and joy-filled team at NYU Langone who performed open-heart surgery on Oak as I was taking on this book. You gave me hope.

To my writers in cahoots: Sarah N., thank you for the couch conversations in Park Slope and the first reads all the way in Colorado. Thank you, Erin, for the endless guidance and friendship.

And to my girlfriends, who have supported me and shared so much with me, from fourteen years of friendship to just only a year or so, there are way too many of you to name, but you are all the wheels behind how women run today and every day. I am so inspired by all of you.

Finally, to my readers and followers, thank you for joining me on this path. Thank you. Thank you!

189

Photo credits

Photography by Bee Walker: pages 6, 8, 9, 10, 12, 23, 24–25, 36, 37, 41, 46, 56, 62, 64, 66, 68, 71, 76, 85, 87 (bottom), 88–89, 92, 95, 100, 110–111, 114, 116, 117, 118, 119, 121, 126, 136–137, 139, 142, 144, 145, 146, 147, 149, 154, 169, 186

Courtesy of the author: page 15 (bottom left), 17, 18 (top, middle, and bottom right), 19, 21 (top), 30, 32, 34, 50, 54, 55, 108, 130 (bottom), 132, 133, 156, 158, 159, 161, 162, 164, 174

Courtesy of Margaret "Peggy" Baker: pages 15 (top left and right), 21 (middle, bottom left and right), 28, 48, 78, 81, 83, 87 (top), 102, 104, 106, 128, 130 (top), 132, 134

Julia Hirsche: 18 (left)

Amanda Petersen: page 35

Julia Robbs: page 26

Editor: Sarah Massey
Designer: Heesang Lee
Production Manager: Michael Kaserkie

Library of Congress Control Number: 2018936284

ISBN: 978-1-4197-3294-2
eISBN: 978-1-68335-496-3
B&N Edition ISBN: 978-1-4197-3993-4

ABRAMS The Art of Books
195 Broadway, New York, NY 10007
abramsbooks.com